YOUR PIECE OF THE PIE

YOUR PIECE OF THE PIE
How to Operate at Greatness

DR. C. S. WILSON

Trilogy Christian Publishers A Wholly Owned Subsidiary of Trinity Broadcasting
Network 2442 Michelle Drive Tustin, CA 92780

Rights Department, 2442 Michelle Drive, Tustin, CA 92780.
Trilogy Christian Publishing/ TBN and colophon are trademarks of Trinity Broad-
casting Network.
For information about special discounts for bulk purchases, please contact Trilogy
Christian Publishing.
Trilogy Disclaimer: The views and content expressed in this book are those of the
author and may not necessarily reflect the views and doctrine of Trilogy Christian
Publishing or the Trinity Broadcasting Network.
Manufactured in the United States of America
10 9 8 7 6 5 4 3 2 1
Library of Congress Cataloging-in-Publication Data is available.
B-ISBN#: 978-1-64773-368-1
E-ISBN#: 978-1-64773-369-8

My fellow cofounders of AireTech Holdings, LLC, the businessaires,
Aire Javon Watson, Aire Travis Wilson, and Aire Brian Wilson

CONTENTS

PREFACE

The proverbial piece of the pie. It's an American saying denoting a share of the nation's wealth, that forty acres and a mule. It's the "general welfare" of the US Constitution.

God has constituted a piece of the pie for His citizens. He wants them to have their piece of significance, their place of success, and their part in satisfaction. He's not authorizing materialism. He knows that a slice of pie for you doesn't mean one less for me. There's a piece of greatness for us all!

This book is about that pie (the one you get) and the biblical pie (the one you take). The latter gets you the former. It will cause you to acquire new strategies, access the favor of God, and position you for miracles. This pie is God's plan for your optimal life. It's why king David prayed, "You shall increase my greatness, and comfort me on every side" (Psalm 71:21 NKJV). He had some of the latter pie.

You don't have to be as smart as Bill Gates or Warren Buffet to be great. You just have to make optimal decisions like them and King David. Let's get you your piece of the pie so you can get your piece of the pie!

ACKNOWLEDGMENTS

My parents, Pastors William and Terry Wilson.

My siblings, Nikki, and Mike Reed,

William, and Mia Wilson Jr.,

Sherika, and Monzo Martin.

My pastor, Reginald Fitzgerald.

My prophet, Sueliman Woodard.

My bishop, Dr. Michael Penn.

GREATNESS:
SIGNIFICANT, SUCCESSFUL, SATISFIED

You shall increase my greatness, and comfort me on every side.
—Psalm 71:21 (NKJV)

As a kid, I ate a lot of pie when I could get away with it. Pie for breakfast, pie for lunch, and pie for dinner. I like a cherry or apple pastry, but my preferred pie is a New York-style pizza pie. I still love an extra cheese, extra pepperoni personal pan pie with garlic butter lightly brushed over its piping hot surface. I'm health conscious now, so I don't do it as often, but I still enjoy getting some of that pie.

Recently I caught a glimpse of a Pizza Hut commercial. They were showing some of their delectable, world-famous pies when their spokesperson broke in "go for greatness...make it great." I remember slightly smiling; I kind of liked it. What an audacious statement. I'm already one of their customers, but the nerve of them! They were claiming that greatness was within my grasp. All I had to do was get one of their delicious pies.

Pizza Hut's courageous campaign is ingenious. They are aware that greatness is alluring and captivating. People are drawn to greatness. People like President Abraham Lincoln, Henry Ford, Martin Luther King Jr., and Oral Roberts intrigue the masses because greatness is associated with them.

You were born to be great in your own right. Not average. The average don't make history. They are soon forgotten in its pages. No one would knowingly vote for a second-rate president. No one remembers the average car designer. No one asks the mediocre public speaker to lead their civil rights movement. No one travels to hear a fair-preaching preacher. Who likes average pizza? No one! But greatness is voted for. It is remembered, it is asked for, it is appealing, and it is appetizing.

OPTIMAL LIVING

It's not just Pizza Hut but PlayStation and other large companies are throwing the word *greatness* around in their advertising. What are they saying? What does it mean to be great? There are seventeen different descriptions for "great" in the *American Heritage College Dictionary*. They include "remarkable or outstanding in magnitude, degree, or extent. Significant, important, chief, noble, excellent. Powerful, influential, eminent, distinguished, grand, aristocrat, and skillful." It can describe a product or a person. It is what you dreamed of when you were a kid. Whether it was a sports star, a doctor, or an astronaut, you dreamed of excelling at it.

When you're operating at greatness, the maximum amount of people will benefit from your remarkable, outstanding decisions, and the least amount of people will be sorrowed by your importance. That's because the great make optimal decisions.

An optimal decision is one that produces the most favorable, advantageous fruit. Everybody's not going to agree with every decision you make. You can't account for everybody, but so long as the maximum amount of people have benefited and the least amount of people sorrowed, you've made the right decision.

You're not for everyone. Your personality won't mix with everyone around you. Your humor won't be funny or understood by everyone. But somebody's going to benefit from being around and/or knowing you. You have a maximum amount of people to influence and a minimum amount to sadden. There's a group of people who will love you and a group that you will never win over. Don't lose any sleep over them; you're not assigned to them.

Everybody has an optimal assignment, but everybody won't pay the price to be upgraded to that rarefied, chief, principle air of optimal decision-making. It doesn't happen automatically. If it did, there would be no mediocrity or greatness spectrum. All would be mediocre; that is average (where most people are).

There is always going to be somebody who is more significant to you than others. Their weight in your life is heavier than others. It could be a parent, sibling, friend, boss, or coworker. The car wash owner needs skilled custodian maintenance workers. A remarkable friend, cook, or preacher wouldn't do them any good during their work hours. They are only valuable to those who need their skill set.

We don't have to be limited by our current skill set. We can all be more "remarkable, outstanding, significant, important, meaningful, superior, noble, excellent, powerful, influential, eminent, distinguished, grand, aristocrat, and skillful" in every area of our lives. That's greatness, no matter who or what it's on or how it's expressed. Greatness describes the best quality available.

I'm not talking about perfectionism. Don't wait to take a risk when everything is perfect. No, write the play, start the business, record the album, bake the cake. God will make it great for somebody. It doesn't have to be the best to everybody; it just has to be the best to somebody. Continue, and an optimal way to proceed will emerge. Eventually, it will become the best to your maximum amount of people.

GREATNESS THE GENIUS OF GOD

Now all those considered great down here by the masses are not necessarily considered great in heaven. Only those who make true optimal decisions because they know God make heaven's great list. You may do a lot of good and look good to a lot of people, but heaven knows how many more people who could have benefited if you had done things differently. The question then is how many people did you help compared to how many you could have helped? That's great reasoning. It's not bad or blameworthy. Greatness is not secular or evil; it's actually an expression of the genius of God. It's how His children can have and be the best to and for the world—the best families, the best businesses, and the best, most vibrant personalities. It causes us to be sought-after to solve earth's perplexing problems because we're excelling at the right things, at the right places, at the right times.

DANIEL THE GREAT

The prophet Daniel was sought after. He was employed by King Belshazzar as a counselor. There was no one quite like him. He had the ability to "interpret dreams, solve mysteries, explain puzzles" (Dan. 5:12 MSG). There were other counselors who interpreted dreams, solved mysteries, and explained puzzles, but none of them excelled at it like Daniel did. When you wanted the best advice in the land, you got word to the prophet Daniel. He excelled at the right thing (giving counsel), at the right place (the king's palace), at the right time (during King Belshazzar's reign).

Daniel had a par excellent spirit. He was above average. He was driven to God, diplomatic with the king's people, and detached from anything that would offend both God and the king's people. Excellent spirited people are as follows:

- *Driven* to God. They are inspired to continue, to do a few optimal tasks daily as bricks in the wall of greatness; *Diplomatic*, able to negotiate, to understand others' personalities, weaknesses, and character flaws, to communicate with compassion and create "win wins"; and
- *Detached* from offending both God and people. They display a keen sense of when to disengage and de-stress. They have broken away from the average mindset.

DESIRABLE

Jesus—the most driven, diplomatic, and detached man—was desirable. My favorite title for Him is "the desire of all nations" (Haggai

2:7 NKJV). This title reveals that He is the ultimate craving of all the nations. Everyone alive is actually craving Him, whether they discern it or not. We think we need a new mate, another car, or plastic surgery. We're so contaminated. We're seeking to fill a void that only He can. He put a desire in us for Him that only He can satisfy. All the presents, power, positions, and prestige won't satisfy for long. Society is acting out with all manners of sin against God because their lives are empty. The God hole is vacant. They're made to please the very one they're hurting. The question for the believer is, "Can I live in such a way that makes Him desirable to those hurting Him?" What does my joy say about Him? My peace? My patience with other believers, and the world? What about my hygiene? My appearance? My work ethic? Does anybody desire Him because of me?

He's longing to display His desirableness. He wants His children to be desirable because of His presence in them. He wants us to succeed. I'm not talking about simple success, the generic kind you read about in magazines and self-help books. You can be successful without being great, but you cannot be great without being successful. I'm talking about true greatness that encompasses success. When God gets the most glory (honor or praise), you're the most impactful and the most fulfilled. That's greatness, eternal success, the life He wants us to acquire and maintain. Saint John said, "It's not possible for a person to succeed—I'm talking about eternal success—without heaven's help" (John 3:27 MSG).

IT'S UP TO YOU

Heaven wants us to operate at greatness. When God gets the most glory, you're the most impactful, and you're the most fulfilled. Said another way, heaven wants us to be the most significant, the most successful, and the most satisfied.

- *Significance* is God's delight in you. It's your value to Him. Your character.

- *Success* is others delight in you. It's your value to them (your achievements). Your conduct.
- *Satisfaction* is your self-delight. It's your self-value. Your contentment.

Operating at greatness bears significant, successful, satisfying fruit. Jesus said, "Herein is my Father glorified that you bear much fruit: so shall you be My disciples" (John 15:8 NKJV). God will get the most glory when you're bearing meaningful, superior, distinguished fruit in every area of your life! Sadly, we drift in and out of greatness situationally and seasonally. For example, you may be satisfied with your position. You make enough money to support your lifestyle, but you're not as successful as you could be because you only do enough to get by. Or you may be succeeding on your job. You just got a raise, but you're not valued by the maximum amount of people because of your arrogant attitude. Greatness eludes us if we don't make significant, successful, satisfying decisions.

If you're not as impactful and fulfilled as you would like to be, then look at how much glory God is getting out of your decisions. Your greatness is predicated on God getting the most glory out of your life. It's up to you.

SUPERIOR QUALITY

Heaven is looking to enlarge the circle of the great, those with recognizable superior qualities. When comparisons are made with in a category (counsel, work, travel, dinning facility, or divinity), there's a difference on the great. David looked at other so-called gods and posted, "I too give witness to the greatness of God, our Lord, high above all other gods" (Psalm 135:5 MSG). He noticed that God our Lord was clearly superior to the other deities. He alone excels at being supreme. To be great is to be better in some aspect than others who are doing the same thing. The word that David used for greatness is *gadol*. It means great in any sense that is better in some way.

You may own a pizza restaurant, but you'll only be great if you can be better in some sense than the other restaurants. It may be your prices, the environment you provide, the size of your product, the hospitality you show, or the delivery of your product. You must have a niche. The great excel at the things that the mediocre has looked over or chosen to ignore. Not identifying where to excel has forfeited their greatness. Whatever your life's occupation, be eminent and distinguished in it.

We are designed to be distinguishable and to desire the better things in life. That is the best products and services because we are the best of creation! We are the apex of God's dream world. Jesus said, "I come so they can have real, and eternal life, more and better life than they ever dreamed of" (John 10:10 MSG).

THE REAL GOD

God is "more and better" than we have the capacity to dream of. Other so-called gods are not like Him. He's better at being God than they've ever been. They can't do what He can. David said of them, "They have mouths, but they do not speak; eyes they have, but they do not see. They have ears, but they do not hear; nor is there any breath in their mouths" (Psalm 135:16–17 NKJV). You can listen for counsel from these gods, but they're not saying anything. You can desire to be noticed by them, but they can't see you. You can cry out to them, but you'll only feel ignored because they cannot hear you.

They can't make anything happen. They are only pleasing to the eyes because they are "the work of men's hands" (Psalm 125:15 NKJV). They were designed to appear to be alive and powerful, but they are the creation of the very people who need their help.

But the God of the Bible is the real God, the qualified CEO of heaven and earth. He is constantly, comprehensively speaking to everybody. He also sees and hears everything coherently all the time. He is alive. "All honor and glory to God forever and ever! He is the eternal king, the unseen one who never dies; He alone is God. Amen" (1 Timothy 1:17 NLT). The greatness of God is without question because He's immortal, invisible (beyond our ability to picture), and eternal. He's better in every way compared to the other deities.

A new pair of shoes, a TV, or a diamond ring can be enjoyable. There's nothing wrong with having them, but many of us make gods of them. We live to obtain them (that's worship). We fill powerful and prestigious when we accumulate them. Our value is derived from having them. Possessions are on the throne of our hearts, and we deify whatever our heart enthrones.

We often look to relationships, houses, cars, clothes, jewelries, jobs, electronics, and money to fill the God void in our lives. We make them gods even though we know that they are limited by time, space, and intelligence. They can't satisfy us for long, but we are often comforted by what we see. We can't see God, but we can be comforted by His mighty good acts. We can sing with King David, "How great is your goodness…" (Psalm 31:19 NKJV). This Hebrew word for great is *rahv*. Strong's dictionary defines it as "abundant, many large in number; of major importance; chief, weighty, significant, noble, and princely." This word implies many in number or significance because having this kind of person or thing is like having many things or people attempting to do the same thing.

Being great takes the place of the masses; it makes large numbers unnecessary. Said another way, great people are important because to equal what they bring to the table, you need a large number of not-so-great people. That's why in the NBA, once a team acquires a franchise player, they rarely trade him because you can't get the same value in return. The franchise player is considered great, so if he's ever traded, the team would receive three or four not-so-great players in an attempt to fill the void.

God illustrates this beautifully. He is the greatest; as such, you need all the money, material things, and technology to come close to imitating Him. You have to bring all that man has to the table to scratch the surface of His greatness. You still can't fill His void!

Without Him, sorrows abound. With Him, blessings abound. For "the blessing of the Lord makes one rich, and adds no sorrow with it" (Proverbs 10:22 NKJV). When the maximum amount of people are being blessed and the minimum amount are sorrowed because of me, then I'm being like Father God.

God's great goodness is clearly seen all around us. We can say with David, "Your marvelous doings are headline news; I could write a book full of the details of your greatness" (Ps. 145:6 MSG). Excellence is print worthy. It solicits the attention of others. You'll be the headline in someone's life when you excel at the right thing (job, family, a sport, an invention, etc.), at the

- right place (in a cubicle, on an assembly line, on stage in a church, etc.), and at the
- right time (when the right person is helped).

That's greatness! It's a part of God's nature. He always excels at the right things, at the right places, and at the right times. The maximum amount of people are always benefiting from His magnitude, and the minimum amount of people are sorrowed by His importance. He never denies Himself glory, impact, or fulfillment. He is maximally significant, successful, and satisfied!

Saint Paul tells us "to be imitators of God as dear children" (Eph. 5:1 NKJV). God wants us to mimic His greatness the way a little boy tries to walk and talk just like his daddy. We must do more than just admire our great Father; we must be inspired to imitate Him. As an excellent dad, He wants greatness for His kids as any great parent would. He wants us to be greater than we even want for ourselves. He desires us to be "exceedingly, abundantly above all that we ask or think" (Ephesians 5:20 NKJV).

Imitating Him is His plan for His glory. The greater you are, the more glory He gets.

DELETE DISCOMFORT

One of the ways that we imitate God is when we delete others' discomfort. The great bring comfort with them to the table. Diplomatically, they find the delete button in distasteful dilemmas. You are only valuable to others when you can remove their discomfort. Whether you're a mechanic, fast-food worker, office clerk, assistant, politician, or a truck driver, the continuous removal of discomfort by solving problems makes you great.

God is known as the "God of all comfort" (2 Corinthians 1:3 NKJV). He is the master at deleting discomfort. To deal with God is to engage a discomfort dispeller. Not only is He aware of all discomfort, He knows how and when to remove them. That's why when God's presence is manifested at church, there is peace (calmness) and joy (bliss). He fans "dis-ease" away. What is the room like when you show up? Is there peace and joy at the anticipation of your presence? What is the room like when you leave? Is it enlightened and sad that you're leaving or excited because you're finally gone? God imitators inject comfort into the atmosphere.

I know we have to keep some discomforts. Pain is a motivator. You don't snatch a toddler out of kindergarten because they are uncomfortable. They must embrace their discomfort for a season. They'll stop crying eventually and adapt.

It's just in the kid as it is in us all to be comfortable. We just have to know when and how to delete our discomforts. You must know what discomforts to nurture. For example, exercise and living by faith. Hard work and having faith won't always be comfortable, but if you embrace them, they enable a comfortable life.

Ultimately, it is the pain of not having greatness that has to be dispelled. You have to despise mediocrity. Then you'll be able to humbly embrace learning and growing. Maturing is not always comfortable, but it is always rewarding. That's part of being great.

Remember, greatness is not ungodly. God wants it for His children. Greatness is a standard. The pizza pie is prepared well or it isn't! The bed is comfortable or it's not! You're living a great life or you're not! It's simple.

HUMBLE DRIVE

The road to greatness is paved with humility. Humble Drive is the only road to a sustained significant, successful, satisfied life. Humility Avenue has to be taken before you can arrive at greatness. We've just done a poor job identifying the road. There was a time when Jesus's closest disciples didn't associate humility with greatness. They wanted the power to be like Jesus, a position that others would know they were like Jesus, and the prestige that comes with having the powerful position. They needed to be pointed to that inconspicuous road.

One day, "the disciples came to Jesus and asked, 'who is the greatest in the kingdom of heaven?'" (Matthew 18:1 NIV). They were expressing their God-given desire to increase. Yet their desire was unbalanced. They wanted to be the greatest, not just one of the greats in the kingdom. They had an unhealthy desire to be recognized, to be honored as CEOs. They wanted to be in the spotlight even though Solomon had warned them, "Don't work your way into the spotlight. Don't push your way into the place of prominence" (Proverbs 25:6 MSG). Social media only makes mainstream what has always been in the hearts of men, the unrestrained desire for prominence.

Be careful not to lust after greatness. Don't be consumed with obtaining it. You'll disconnect from principles and the integrity you'll need to sustain it. Beware of overly ambitious, spotlight-driven people with no genuine concern for anyone other than themselves.

To curb the disciples' unchecked lust for prominence, Jesus demonstrated a very important truth. "He called a little child and had him stand among them" (Matthew 18:2 NIV). This engaged their vision. The kid would serve as a walking memorial commemorating what Jesus was about to teach them. This lesson would be in the earth as long as children are. They would serve to trigger their memory of this moment. He doesn't want them to forget what they are about to hear because it would be needed in every season of their lives.

I can picture the disciples listening attentively, thinking Jesus was going to give them some instructions in childcare since they were so trustworthy. Maybe He wanted them to mentor the next generation. Surely, they were not about to learn from a kid's attitude? Jesus began explaining, "I tell you the truth, unless you change and become like little children, you will never enter the kingdom of heaven" (Matthew 18:3). He answers a question that they had not asked. They wanted to know how to be big shots in the kingdom, but He told them what they assumed they knew. That is, how to get into the kingdom of heaven.

He was highlighting the importance of humility by showing them that they must first possess it like a child before they could even enter the kingdom of heaven. Kids don't care about power, positions, or prestige. At the end of the day, you must have a child's approach to life to be and stay great. They were now forced to rethink who would have greatness in God's kingdom. Using this standard, greatness could be accessed by anybody. No one person had to be the greatest alone. Significance, success, and satisfaction is for anyone who will get low enough to have it.

He continued, "Therefore, whoever humbles himself like this child is the greatest in the kingdom of heaven" (Matthew 18:4). They kid He put among them was a part of earth's illustration of real greatness. It was awesomely profound yet amazingly simple. Profound because He had just given them the key to greatness, and simple because it was easy to understand. It leveled the playing field for all of mankind. You want greatness? You must be responsible for knowing humility's role in every season and scene of your life. It is always on the great to some degree and in some form. Humbleness comes before greatness.

Now don't picture one of our little sassy seven- or eight-year-olds. This demonstration would have been clearly understood because a child during that time, the first century AD, didn't have the technology that our kids have today. There was no internet, cable TV, tablets, or smartphones desensitizing them to disrespect, dishonor, and death. They were not exposed to things that only adults who don't know God should see and hear. These kids were innocent and dependent upon their parents for protection and provision. They were less likely to be spoiled and feel entitled. These children were free to be kids without the responsibility of their own greatness. In that era, parents would transfer their occupation and set the worldview of their children. A great parent would raise a great child.

Jesus's message was clear; kingdom kids are to be innocent and dependent upon their heavenly Father to protect and provide for them. They should put their trust in Him and receive their occupation and worldview from Him. This trust in Him allows us to live free and empowers Him to be responsible for the greatness He wants us to have.

The disciples were told to be committed to being humble. That in brokenness and meekness they were to persistently seek to be child-like. He doesn't mind that they wanted to be great; He put the desire in them. Yet when it surfaces, it comes through tainted vessels, so He had to balance their approach.

Author Eugene Peterson paraphrased Christ's words as, "I'm telling you once and for all, that unless you return to square one and start over like children, you're not even going to get a look at the kingdom, let alone get in. Whoever becomes simple and elemental again, like this child, will rank high in God's Kingdom" (Matt. 18:3–4 MSG). Jesus told us once and for all to take the lowly road like children do. They start their childhood over every day. They do not hold on to anger and wrongs from yesterday; they don't overthink life. Every day starts from the low place. Humility Avenue kids usually stay on that road. They're fairly *driven, diplomatic,* and *detachable* until they're tainted by the world (and puberty). Eventually they start to think they know more than their parents.

In the same way as God's kids imitate His greatness by not holding on to anger and wrongs from yesterday, we shouldn't overthink this life of trusting in Him. We should start every day prepared to encounter life from Humble Drive forever and always. We should never think that we know better than God leaving the low place. Greatness awaits all those who are not above learning from a child to practice the discipline of returning to brokenness boulevard every day. It will bring greatness to you. Not it might, it will. That's Father God's way.

In that scene, Jesus excelled at the right thing (teaching on humility), at the right place (outside where the children were), and at the right time (in Saint Matthew's presence, who would later record it). The maximum amount of people are benefitting (the readers of the book of Matthew), and the minimum amount of people are sorrowed (those who haven't read the book of Matthew).

JESUS THE GREAT

Jesus's disciples listened to everything He had to say. He was the truth; everything He taught them was right. When it came to greatness, they asked Jesus about it because He was the greatest they had ever seen. They wanted to know how to have that status among themselves and their peers.

God's glory, extensive impact, and personal fulfillment characterized Jesus's life. Saint Luke wrote a book about His life, and the first thing he recorded about him after giving his name was "He will be great" (Luke 1:32 NKJV). Luke's announcement put the world on notice that it was about to host greatness. This soon became evident when He arrived because He was superb at everything He set out to do. He was and is a "great prophet" (Luke 7:16 NKJV), a "great shepherd" (Hebrews 13:20 NKJV), and a "great high priest" (Hebrews 4:14 NKJV).

Every decision that Jesus the Great made bore the most favorable advantageous fruit. That's because He made all His optimal decisions from Humble Drive. Let's discover its place in you getting your piece of the pie—a great mind, great vision, great leadership, a great career, great faith, a great life, great power, a great deliverance, and great wealth.

JESUS ON HUMILITY AVENUE

There was incapacitating greatness emanating from the hem of His priestly garments! He was the greatest and the humblest; the former was because of the latter. Willingly coming to earth from heaven is the greatest act of humility ever. And rising from the dead and ascending back into heaven was the greatest accomplishment ever. I heard Dr. James Merritt say that "we spend our whole lives trying to climb the ladder; Jesus spent His coming down it." No extensive self-promotion campaign; it was all God's promotion. He told His disciples that he was "humble and gentle at heart" (Matthew 11:29 NLT). That was the only description of Himself that He gave.

He could have told them how great He was at prophesying, shepherding, and being the God-man. He would not have been lying if He told them how in eternity past He had "created the heavens and the earth" (Genesis 1:1 NKJV) in six days. How "all things were made by Him and without Him nothing was made that was made" (John 1:3 NKJV). He could have proclaimed how He never made not one suboptimal decision, but He never did.

Had the disciples been paying close enough attention, they would have seen that Jesus didn't move a muscle in pride. He was never full of Himself. He lived His life so "that the Father may be glorified" in Him "the Son" (John 14:13 NKJV). They should have discerned this when He told them, "I can of Myself do nothing. As I hear, I judge; and my judgment is righteous because I do not seek My own will but the will of the Father who sent me" (John 5:30 NKJV). He lived to do what Father God wanted Him to, which was evidence that He was always on Humility Avenue. He was driven to accomplish His assignment (what He heard the Father say and what He saw the Father do). He was diplomatic with His contemporaries, and He was detached from the lust and fears of the world.

LOOK AT THE CROSS

His assignment led to the worst kind of execution in the history of the world—death by suffocating on a cross. Breathing was restricted because the chest cavity was forcibly expanded. The cross delayed death until the maximum amount of torture had been inflicted. Unlike the swift death of an electric chair or a poisonous injection, this was cruel and unusual punishment. Relentless, excruciating pain throbbed his body as he grasped for air. When He was nailed to the cross, He was already in critical condition because He was beaten earlier that day. In His last moment of life, He dropped His head, exhaling His final breath. Jesus was at His lowest point, but with God, your lowest point in life qualifies you to be your greatest! You don't qualify to be your greatest until you've been your lowest.

He was propelled from this horrific death to the greatest position in the heavens—the right hand of God the Father. As awful as His death was at that moment, God was getting the most glory. He was the most impactful, and He was the most fulfilled. Do not worry about what your greatness will look like. Commit to humbleness, and God will make you eternally successful to the maximum amount of people.

God took what would have been the scene of the biggest defeat in history, and He made the cross an emblem of hope for mankind. God specializes in the hard cases. No one had ever come back from death by way of a cross before. The cross was undefeated. Yet because Jesus was doing what the Father told him to, God caused greatness to surface from His dead situation. God wants to do the same for all of His children who are willing to trust Him to do it for them. He set a precedence that no situation is too far gone. As long as there is breath in your body, there is greatness awaiting your soul. Don't base what God is going to do for you on the experience of others. Their life's crucifixion may have suffocated them, but God wants to set precedence for His children.

ETERNAL SUCCESS

I believe the cross itself demonstrates God's desire for us. It consists of a vertical beam that is slightly longer than its intersecting horizontal beam. Its proportions make it the lethal execution weapon that it is. It's not a T or an X. It's a cross. Historically, that symbol has served as the axis on any grid representing heaven and earth. It was fitting that the Creator of heaven and earth would save the world by defeating the cross which represented all of heaven and earth. Since then, the cross has been pointing to the possibility of obtaining any level of greatness that you want with your priorities. Like Jesus, humble yourself before Father God (vertical beam points to God), then humble yourself before man (horizontal beam points to man). Prioritize your relationship with God first, then your relationships with men. Be driven to God, then diplomatic with man. Most people don't heed the way of the cross. They manipulate their way through life (long horizontal beams). Then when they are in trouble or transition, they acknowledge God (short vertical beams). They have inverted crosses. The cross you adhere to determines your eternal success. What cross does your priorities follow? If I was a fly on your wall or if I could listen in on your phone conversations, what would your relationships tell me?

INCREASED GREATNESS

I wonder what it would have been like to follow King David around. He had some measure of success and significance. He had killed the Philistine giant, Goliath. That gained him some recognition. Then we read that "in Hebron, he reigned over Judah seven years and six months" (2 Samuel 5:5 NKJV). He went on to reign over all of Israel in Jerusalem when the Bible says, "David went on to become great" (2 Samuel 5:10 NKJV). He was accomplished, but God had more for David to achieve, more in front of him to attain. Never become satisfied with your current state of significance. Stay in self-discovery, trying new things, developing new skills, and meeting new people. There are more lives to impact for the kingdom. Somebody is waiting on you to excel, to go on and become great.

Humility increases your greatness. Wanting God to be glorified more through him, the king prayed, "You shall increase my greatness and comfort me on every side" (Psalm 71:2 NKJV). That's a desire that rests in the bosom of the Father-in-Chief—to increase our comfort (satisfaction) on every side.

David was requesting this increase from Humble Drive, from what he called "the depths of the earth" where he was experiencing "severe troubles" (Psalm 71:20 NKJV). I don't know exactly what he was going through, but his humility there qualified him to hit the ceiling of greatness on his life. He cried out from his lowest, so he was qualified to be his greatest.

David went on to reign in Jerusalem for "thirty-three years over all Israel and Judah" (2 Samuel 5:5 NKJV). He became significant to more people. Even though he was flawed, his commitment to stay on Humble Drive kept him positioned to ride into more and more greatness. There's more territory for you to be king over, more people for you to influence, and more systems for you to conquer.

I love the old story of a certain young British man who grew up in poverty. He never knew any of the finer things in life. Thus, it was no surprise when he found himself in trouble for stealing. He was just eighteen years old, facing hard time for stealing sheep. He would swoop in at night and lead the unsuspecting, defenseless sheep away. He was convicted and sentenced to two years in the penitentiary.

Great Britain had a legal practice back then that after a criminal was convicted, they would engrave the initials of the crime on their forehead. Being that the young man was a sheep thief, a large "S.T." was seared right into the crease on his forehead. He was branded for life!

While in prison, however, the young lad became a Christian. His new passion now was converting and discipling men for the Lord Jesus. At twenty years old, he was released. Not wanting to disturb the wounds of any of his victims, he swallowed his pride and moved to the next town over. There he served faithfully in the church as an evangelist and a teacher. Now many men (sheep) were saved and strengthened because of him. This went on for the next forty years until he died.

During his memorial service, some of the men who had been touched by his ministry posed a question, "What did that 'S.T.' on his forehead stand for?" Doing their time with him, it never came up. One English man who knew him for some thirty years exclaimed that he "never heard of him doing anything wrong." It must stand for "saint," for he was truly a great man. He had been making optimal decisions for forty years!

That young Britain had increased his greatness through the years. His past paled in comparison to where he ended. I want you to know that your past pales in comparison to where the Lord wants to take you. It's not too late to change the narrative of your life. God can be glorified through you. You can be more impactful and more fulfilled. You can have your piece of significance, your place of success, and your part in satisfaction.

The young Britain humbled himself, leaving the comforts of his hometown to serve the Lord in another town. Are you willing to travel to increase? What price are you willing to pay to operate at greatness?

YOUR PIECE OF THIS PIE

Some people take a fork into the pie but are too lazy
to raise it to their mouth.
—Proverbs 19:24 (MSG)

Some five hundred years ago when most of the known world hosted kingdoms, things were much simpler than they are now. Adults worked, took care of their responsibilities at home, and paid taxes to their king. They didn't have the variety of entertainment that we have today (smartphones, tablets, movie theaters, theme parks, etc.). They enjoyed the simpler things like nature, social interactions, and family meals.

Humble pie was a common dish at these family meals. It consisted of deer organs and breaded crust. When the king's hunters had killed some deer, the best part of the game was brought to the king's cooks—the breast, hindquarters, and ribs. The less desirable unappetizing parts were discarded—liver, intestines, kidneys, and the heart. Excited about the waste, the common people would gather them and prepare themselves a meal.

These discarded organs were known as the "humbles" because they were not as valuable as the other animal parts. The pheasants would carefully bake these leftover organs, then place them in a shale made of flower and water. This pie was eaten regularly by the common people, but you would never find this dish on the king's imperial table. The king had the pick of the land to feast on. All the sweet fruits, delicious vegetables, and prime meat he wanted. For him to eat humble pie would mean that he didn't reign over much. The average family ate it because they weren't afforded many options. They were considered lower-class citizens. After harsh taxes, land that didn't fully cooperate, animals that didn't produce, or having to feed multiple children, many families were forced to eat the pie. Eating it was a reminder that your life was subpar, and it conveyed to others that you were not a part of the king's cabinet. Your diet was an indication of your social status.

Back then, they ate the pie because their circumstances made them. Thus, when someone was forced to do something that they didn't necessarily want to such as admit some fault or apologize for a mistake, they would be said to have eaten some "humble pie." Just as the common folk of a few hundred years ago wasn't in love with having to eat humble pie, no one today enjoys not being able to "save face." That's because being made to eat a slice of humble pie leaves you no room to be prideful. It equates to swallowing your pride, deleting any vainglory, arrogance, haughtiness, or pompousness.

We can all recall a time when we've been made to eat from that proverbial pastry. Those experiences are distasteful because nobody likes being embarrassed or put to shame no matter who it's in front of or how temporary it may be. Nobody likes being put in their place because it conveys the fact that something is wrong with us; we don't have it all together.

In this book, we are subtracting the forcefulness from this common description of humble pie. For our purposes, we will be using it to mean humility itself, the state of being humble, to persevere yet be meek and broken at the same time. The humble have the right attitude that stems from the right estimation of self. I'm talking about being "the willing humble" (James 4:6 MSG), not having to be made to lower yourself. In taking away the involuntary admission of wrong, we'll see that it is the only pie that you can eat daily that's good for you. It's true; you are what you eat. This dish is no different. You must eat your way to greatness! Humility precedes greatness. Many don't associate this exclusive virtue with greatness because the wide misconception of what it actually is. The fallacy surrounding humility contributes to why it is the most overlooked agent in the greatness equation, but when unveiled, it can usher you into your destiny. A desire for this dish is certain to follow anyone who fully grasp this delicacy's majestic nature.

THE IMITATION PIE

Many are "puffed up with the wrong kind of ingredient" (1 Corinthians 5:7 MSG). An imitation pie. Like being a passive doormat that's not real humbleness. It's not fragile or weak, lacking strength and courage. The humble are always ready when progression is needed for growth on the individual and organizational level. It's not silent and reserved when communication is necessary just to appear humble. This is what the Bible calls "false humility" (Colossians 2:23 NKJV), humility without wisdom. It is an imitation pie that appears to be real like a fruit basket centerpiece on a kitchen table. It looks good, but you can't do anything with it.

To reap the foreseeable benefits of being considerate and modest, we put on this false humility. This way, we don't have to be committed to working on our character. False humility is pretending to have eaten some of the real pie. We get a "fork into the pie" (Proverbs 19:24 MSG), but it's just for show. Like when we give to the Salvation Army Santa Claus who is conveniently stationed outside of Walmart. Not because we had a burning desire to help the less fortunate, but to show that we can afford it or to feel better about ourselves. It appears noble, but no genuine concern is attached to it. It is pretentiousness, "the wrong kind of ingredient" (1 Corinthians 5:7 MSG).

Timidity, shyness, bashfulness, and apprehensiveness overstepping out in faith and taking risk are not characteristics of humility. Indecisiveness and faintheartedness are ungodly. The pie is not made up of low self-esteem, low self-confidence, or the lack of self-assurance. It's not walking around with your head down afraid to speak to other people. The scripture is clear, "God doesn't like us to be shy" (2 Timothy 1:7 MSG). It commands us to "not throw away your confidence. It will be richly rewarded" (Hebrews 10:35 NIV). He wants us to think highly of ourselves. We're just not to think "more highly" (Romans 12:3 NKJV) of ourselves, then we ought to think.

Shyness is just a manifestation of pride. It's being overly concerned with self. Shy people have the wrong estimation of self. You know you're shy if you don't take compliments well. Your boss comple-ments you on a masterful presentation. Instead of accepting it grace-fully, you say "it was not that good" or "I could have done better." Your response takes the attention off the accomplishments and places it solely on you. Pride keeps us in the center. Shy people think of them-selves constantly. God wants us to receive compliments with class. He wants others to "see your good works and glorify your Father in heav-en" (Matthew 5:16 NKJV).

Another one of the mistaken ingredients of the pie is ignorance. Humility is not being uninformed, is not being afraid to ask questions about the things of God, technology skill set, or the social skills that could assist your family, friends, or coworkers. God doesn't want his representatives unaware of his investment in them. Ignorance is not bliss; it brings blisters. It keeps confidence at bay while serving as a magnet for ruin. God's word on it is "my people perish for lack of knowledge" (Hosea 4:6 NKJV). Knowledge deletes perishability. Igno-rance blisters lives.

ONE-PART PERSEVERANCE

Humble pie is made of perseverance, meekness, and brokenness. Perseverance allows you to stay the course, is tenacious and commit-ted to whatever it's assigned to. There is no obstacle or obstruction that it can't overcome. To be humble is to be driven, to be positioned below customary dignity, and to keep going. It's not moved by oppos-ing voices, for it is programmed for progression. The humble won't be denied; they persevere.

In the spring of 2012, I was watching Messianic Rabbi Jona-than Bernis interview Hebrew scholar, Dr. Frank Seekins. Dr. Seek-ins discussed the ancient biblical Hebrew equivalent of our English word *humble*, which is *shach*. He explained that it meant being "flat-on-your-face humble." Shach is made up of two Hebrew words. The first means "teeth, devour, and destroy;" the other means "the fence."

The picture that the Hebrew portrays is one who will devour, destroy, or bite through any fences if necessary. It's a picture of one that perseveres.

A fence is anything that would serve as an enclosure, boundary, or burial that would hinder or prevent your passage. It can be a poverty-stricken neighborhood, a troubled childhood, a mistake-filled pass, an underexposed culture, limited materials, finances, or connections. They, in turn, could cause internal fences to arise such as hopelessness, doubt, depression, fear, envy, strife, or self-aggrandizement. No matter where the fence maybe, external or internal, the humble nature is to come driving through it.

This aspect of humility is often overlooked. The humble is not denied by anyone or anything. They are broken enough to find the way through any opposition. They will get the appropriate tool to destroy the fence that is blocking their advance. As barriers are being built up all around, the humble declares that "what's in me will not let those boundaries stay up and close me in. What's in me won't let any awkwardness stop me from getting to my destiny."

Being this "flat on your face" humble is to be a relentless force, adamant and unstoppable. It doesn't matter how dirty you get while staying the course. It's making yourself "of no reputation" (Philippians 2:7 NKJV). It's resolved to deny defeat. That's why other people's opinions of you are insignificant. Ultimately, you've destroyed the fence of dignity. When any victory is won, humility was there in some form. It is just often unrecognized. This is because it has different forms. The protocol that is needed is the posture that's assumed when the pie has been consumed. If silence is needed, silence is assumed. If it's a word in season, then the word is given. If the table needs to be turned over, then consider it flipped. The humble will go wherever they have to despite how they feel or what their bank account says. They keep repositioning themselves to be triumphant declaring that "God always leads us in triumph in Christ" (Corinthians 2:14 NKJV).

They are driven despite daunting difficulties. This chapter's opening verse speaks to this end. "Some people dig a fork into the pie but are too lazy to raise it to their mouths" (Proverbs 19:24 MSG). They do not persist. There is no power to proceed. Laziness keeps them from following through with the right tasks and responsibilities. They are the haughty. This group does what they want or what can be done with ease—that which possesses no difficulty. They are vain and proud, persisting occasionally but not daily.

Yet the humble will do daily what the haughty only do occasionally. The humble know what they need—the nourishment of the pie every day. Without it, they won't have the fence destroying power they'll need to be significant, successful, and satisfied. It is the consistency of small drops of water that eventually erodes the largest mountain.

Many people lack the discipline to do what it takes daily to cover them to excel because it's easier to watch all the new cable sitcoms and browse the web. That's why most people do it; it's easy. Television and the internet are not bad, but we enjoy more leisure time now than any other time in history! Leisure time won't bring or accommodate the greatness God wants to provide for us. The humble press fear through the daily temptation of immediate gratification. Remember, they do daily what the haughty only do occasionally.

Anybody can read their Bible and pray once in a while. Anybody can have a good attitude every now and then. Anybody can eat a healthy meal once in a blue moon. Anybody can go to bed at a decent time on Sunday night, but what about the rest of the week? Anybody can work on their skill set and personal development occasionally, but what would I find if I followed you around all day for a week? What does your week say about you? Your schedule betrays you; it won't lie for you! Show me your average week's schedule, and I'll tell you who you are and where you're going.

Your schedule is recording your habits. It will tell if you have the perseverance that external success is made of. No matter how hard or monotonous a great routine may be, without perseverance, stubborn fences remain and grow larger. You need to persevere, so when "you have done the will of God, you will receive what He has promised" (Hebrews 10:36 NIV).

To get whatever He promised, you have to persevere.

I've read hundreds of nonfiction books (self-help, spiritual, practical life, business, and biographies). Many had great advice, tips, and strategies for pleasing God, time management, finances, family and career relationships. A lot of bestsellers and must-reads. There is a lot of great information available in print and electronically. Yet perseverance is needed to continue to act on what the respected authors have disclosed. Without it, there can be no lasting improvement, and greatness stays off in the distance because the pie—not the books themselves—empower you to persevere. Wanting us to succeed, Apostle Paul told us to "pray at all times [on every occasion, in every season] in the Spirit, and with this in view, stay alert with all perseverance and petition [interceding in prayer] for all of God's people" (Ephesians 6:18 AMP). He was telling us to be humble enough to keep praying for others, to destroy the fences in their lives. Not everyone is dining on the pie, so they don't have the internal fortitude, the drive they need to persist.

We're to have purposeful persistence, a determined diligence. I tell people to have competent diligence; that is too know what to do and to have the determination to keep doing it. Competence without diligence is wasted talent. Diligence without competence is wasted energy. But like a trail of ants to a bread crumb, competent diligence brings the achievement of your desired end. That's why the Bible says, "Diligence is man's precious possession" (Proverbs 12:27 NKJV). Competent men acquire diligence, also known has perseverance.

ONE-PART MEEKNESS

A more recognizable ingredient of the pie is good old tasty meekness. This is how most people would depict the humble—meek and lowly. The meek are gentle and mild. They have patience with people and systems. Meekness is being calm in the midst of difficulties. It is having the right estimation of self and others; an evaluation that is sober and accurate. It is diplomatic, considerate, and not given to extremes, leading a "quiet and peaceful life in all godliness and reverence" (1 Timothy 2:2 NKJV). The meek do not meddle in affairs that they are not in some way responsible for. They seek to get rid of agitation. They are respectful in all their encounters because they are concerned about the human family. They are not pretentious. There is no pretending to be what you want others to see you as. It's being genuine. You're meek when "you're content with just who you are—no more, no less" (Matthew 5:5 MSG).

There's a Greek word, *tapeinophrosyne*, that's translated in the Bible as humility. *Vine's Complete Expository Dictionary of Old and New Testament Words* defines it using words like "humiliation of mind, modesty, and most genuine self-evaluation." It's this modest and most genuine self-evaluation that our society is missing. It's why the Apostle Paul told the women of his day to "adorn themselves in modest appeal with propriety and moderation" (1 Timothy 2:9 NKJV). He was telling them to properly evaluate themselves, know their worth, and have their clothes reflect their personal assessment. He wanted the women to cherish themselves, so they wouldn't dress like the women who undervalued themselves (namely the prostitutes). We can't think so little or so much of ourselves that we'll put on or do anything. Saint Paul also said, "Develop a sober estimate of yourself based on the standard which God has given to each of you" (Romans 12:3 CJB).

Tapeinophrosyne describes a person without pompousness. They live with their imperfections, so they compassionately relate to others' conditions. They show "unqualified courtesy toward everybody" (Titus 3:2 AMP). They're what great humans are made of—meekness. *Tapeinophrosyne* is made up of two Greek words. The first, *tapeinos* means humble, and the other, *phren* means mind. The picture that the Greek language paints is someone who has a mind that stays humble. They have an internal reset button that puts them in their proper place mentally. Like when someone tries your patience and you think to yourself, "If you had called me a year ago, I would have let you have it." That's internal resetting to keep coming back to "unqualified courtesy" even when it's costly to do so. They don't worry about their feelings; feelings have a way of catching up. A set mind will cause your world's capacity for greatness to skyrocket.

Now knowing the ancient Hebrew picture for humble is one that destroys the fence, then our Greek word would imply one whose mind is perpetually set to destroy, devour, or bite through in an opposing fence. Their mind is set to get through life in the right way. It finds and keeps the right mental approach when money is tight, kids are defiant, or sickness arises. You'll have the calmness of mind to find the solutions.

Meekness causes you to find and utilize a balanced mind. The strive for balance in life is a lifelong struggle that man will always be in. I guarantee you that something in your life is out of balance as you're reading this. No worries. The nature of meekness is to seek out and continue in balance, so your world can thrive. The meek will find the balance in any condition or circumstance. There is a medium in all situations, and that's the resting place of the meek. They live from the best, most beneficial place. What's in them won't let what's around them stay out of balance. Whether it's an unbalanced marriage or other family ties, career relationships, work schedule, diet, or checkbook, the humble mind brings balance where things are in disarray.

This mind isn't assuming but understanding, and it doesn't point fingers. It's what Brother Solomon was describing when he said, "Don't jump to conclusions. There may be a perfectly good explanation for what you just saw" (Proverbs 25:8 MSG). Contrarily, it's the haughty mind that jumps to conclusions. Being high minded, they suppress their imperfections long enough to judge what somebody else is doing. In doing so, they don't make allotments for their own misunderstandings or honest mistakes. We've all judged people because of their clothes, their mannerisms, or the way they spoke. We may not have recognized our haughty thoughts, but they existed nonetheless in our big heads. We have ignored the Bible's charge to have some "humbleness of mind" (Colossians 3:12 KJV).

Meekness is a part of that delicious fruit of the spirit. It is pleasant, delightful, and courteous. It makes one enjoyable and compels people to be around you to soak in your presence. God made you to work optimally with meekness. It's how He wanted to be represented, so His word declares that we should be "shewing all meekness unto all men" (Titus 3:2 KJV). Everyone should get to enjoy this rare virtue, as well as possess it themselves.

ONE-PART BROKENNESS

Now the pie wouldn't be complete without some good old brokenness. Broken—this is the state of being totally dependent upon God to make your life what it is destined to be. To be broken is to give God the glory for everything He does through you. It's living as one that has been subdued by the Lord Jesus Christ, the most broken one. It's being a conquered conqueror, a chained champion who's empowered because he or she is submitted.

Brokenness documents your trust in God so that when you stop trusting in God, it's because you're not broken. But we can't trust ourselves. We don't know why we make some of the decisions we make. Yet brokenness enables you to disengage from the mental anguish, stress, tension, depression, dependency, and defection that comes from trusting in yourself. Brokenness is knowing what not to do and then not doing it. Perseverance enables you to continue implementing the right things. Meekness gets you balanced. Brokenness is the detaching element. To be broken is to give away to the Father's plan for your life. We should be able to echo what Jesus said, "My Father, if there is any way to get me out of this, but please, not what I want. You, what do you want?" (Matthew 26:39 MSG). He was fully aware that what the Father wanted to do with Him would be the best for Him, and it would benefit the maximum amount of people. To be broken is to let God do what's best for you and those who are connected to your life's journey. Your will is limited by what you know and the relationships you have. God has already accounted for everything you don't know and everyone you're going to need. Brokenness closes the distance between your will and God's will.

There is a Hebrew word found multiple times in the Bible for humble that conveys this meaning *shaphel*. Strong's dictionary says that it means "to bring down, to make low, to be broken down." It is usually used figuratively. It's a picture of one being made to let their pride go and dwell in a low place. It can be used to describe one humbling or breaking themselves for a superior intent.

Brokenness is when you willingly break yourself down to a more manageable position. You break away from offending God and man to be more useful, and subsequently more desirable. The best sports coaches (whether basketball, baseball, hockey, or soccer) carry the will of the team, not their own. They manage themselves for team success. They win championships because they put not necessarily what they want first but the schedules and strategies that is best for the team first, the superior intent.

Like an experienced coach, we should let our pride go and dwell in the low place. God inhabits the low places. Just as the broken rose releases the sweet-smelling fragrance, the broken child of God releases a sweet-smelling aroma to the Father. The Bible says, "God is near to those who have a broken heart" (Psalms 34:18 NKJV). Brokenness sounds an alarm in heaven. It brings God close. He enjoys the company of the broken; they are delightful to him and others. It is humanity's most pleasant disposition.

No matter how it is derived, a broken heart is a receptive heart. Brokenness positions you to receive. It accepts instructions and corrections. It is quick to self-correct, to admit a wrong, to ask for forgiveness, and to make restoration if necessary. Whatever area of your life that has dried up (your faith, your career, or your finances), brokenness will release the floods of refreshing water gushing in with needed rejuvenation.

I'm talking about being pliable and flexible as opposed to having a hardened heart that's stubborn, headstrong, and self-willed. That's the hardened life; it comes from forcing your own agenda. It's the life that makes plans without God, so there is no stability. God is the stabilizer, the only constant in an ever-changing world, so if He's not on your team, you won't be poised. He only works with those who are pliable and flexible, those who were striving to be broken, those who have broken away from their own self-will, from their willingness to satisfy their own desires in their own way. You can't trust your will because "the heart is hopelessly dark and deceitful, a puzzle that no one can figure out" (Jeremiah 17:9 MSG). Our hearts are not stable enough to know what's best for us. We need God's help period!Being self-dependent assures that the worst parts of us will be exposed. The worst parts of you will come to the surface—your pride, anger, jealousy, lust, dishonor, hatred, and fears. Brokenness will keep these—the worst parts of you—from destroying you. That's the single greatest thing the Lord has shown me about brokenness. It will keep you from destroying yourself. For example, let's say you have an extremely bad anger problem, a quick temper. You get mad when things don't go your way. Rage is devouring the life that you could have. Well, if you had some brokenness, you wouldn't be enraged as quickly. Less things would upset you and those that do will not cause you to break. You can't break the broken. Yes, brokenness will keep the worse parts of you from destroying you.

Brokenness gives humble pie its impervious nature. When you have the pie, you're not easily pierced. The noise of turmoil and trouble will not penetrate you easily. Great hurt, heartache, and pain that has no right to be inside you permeating your soul and lose its staying power. Your life has been interrupted long enough. Stop sabotaging where you could be, where the pie can take you, and what the pie can make you.

What the Lord Jesus Christ said is true. "It's trouble ahead if you're satisfied with yourself. Yourself will not satisfy you for long period" (Luke 6:25 MSG). Being stuck on yourself ensures a feeling of emptiness. You can't give yourself a satisfaction-guaranteed clause. Feasting on yourself is why you are always hungry and wanting more stuff that will never please you or make you content. How vain and shallow we can be. Brokenness shows us how hollow, aimless, and messed up we are by way of the distance between our will and God's will for us. Only He can satisfy our inner vacancy, and only the broken gets this fulfillment. When it comes to your will, if it ain't broke, then break it.

EAT MORE PIE

Perseverance, meekness, and brokenness combine to make this delicious pie. Perseverance is the driving component in getting you to stay on the God-given course doing His revealed will. Meekness is the diplomatic element taking the most advantageous stance for self and all foreseeable parties involved creating win-win situations. Then brokenness is the discouraging element, the ever detaching from self-sufficiency and of error element. These abilities position you to excel at the right things, at the right places, at the right times. So for God to get more glory out of your life, you have to be more driven, more diplomatic, and more detachable. You have to eat more pie to get your piece of the pie.

All Christians are appealed to by Saint Paul to "walk worthy of the calling with which you were called with all lowliness and gentleness, with long-suffering bearing with one another in love" (Ephesians 4:12 NKJV). To "walk worthy" of the unique call that God has for you is to live your life in such a way that it reflects His character, His thoughts, and His ways. You do this when you're walking in lowliness, gentleness, and long suffering. Compare this charge to the pie's ingredients:

- Lowliness—meekness
- Gentleness—brokenness
- Long suffering—perseverance

The Bible is telling us to have ourselves some humble pie if we want our walk to be considered worthy enough to represent God in the earth. It's the only way. When I'm operating in pride, I expose myself to those around me. I show how undeserving and worthless I am to show God off to them. When I'm humble, I show that I'm in step with God and that I can add value to others.

JESUS: GOT PIE?

Jesus was in step with God. Just look at how he came. He arrived on planet earth as a baby by way of a virgin womb that He created! "When the time came, he set aside the privileges of deity and took on the statue of a slave, became human! Having become human, He stayed human. It was an incredibly humbling process. He didn't claim special privileges. Instead, he lived a selfless, obedient life" (Phil. 2:7 MSG). That's our three ingredients at work.

- "He set aside the privileges of deity and took on the status of a slave and became human" (one-part brokenness).
- "Having become human, He stayed human" (one-part perseverance).
- "He didn't claim special privileges. Instead, He lived a selfless obedient life" (one-part meekness).

He detached Himself from the riches of heaven, He was driven to the Father as a human, and He was diplomatic in His human dealings.

There is no missing the pie's place in Jesus's life. The pie's principle is that greatness comes from humility of which Jesus is the prototype. He will eventually be known by all as "the Master of all" (Philippians 1:11 MSG). He excelled at the right thing (resurrection from death), at the right place (under Roman rule where crucifixion was still practiced), and at the right time (two thousand years ago when Rome's road system made it easy for news to spread).

THE FATHER: GOT PIE?

It is clear how the pie propelled Jesus into greatness among us being the most significant, outstanding human to ever live. At the same time, it's clear that God the Father, "the great God that formed everything" (Prov. 26:10 NKJV), has never put His deity aside, been associated with slaves, or become human. How does the pie's principle apply to Him then? Does humility have a place in the existence of God?

King David sheds some light on our questions. He asks, "Who is like the Lord our God, who dwells on high, who humbles Himself to behold the things that are in the heavens and in the earth?" (Psalms 113:5 NKJV). Rhetorically, he enquires about the greatness of God, "Who is like the Lord our God?" Obviously, no one. He has no rival. Then He declares what's not as obvious—the Father Himself loves the pie. He "humbles" Himself to behold the things that are in the heavens and in the earth.

King David says that God's humbleness is shown in His looking into the affairs of the world. He's the CEO of the universe and all existing things. Earth is just one of the planets in our galaxy, yet God is concerned about the apex of His creation—humans and their environment. He didn't speak the world into existence and then turn His back on it. He's aware of everything that goes on in and around it.

Since He's the highest being in existence, He has to lower Himself to care about us. He's so great that it is an act of humility for Him just to look at us. He only deals with us through humbleness. If He didn't, we would be overwhelmed by His power. Imagine a kid playing with his ant farm. As long as he is present with his creatures, he's willingly limiting himself to behold them. The kid has to be gentle because unrestrained strength could be fatal to the ants. To the ants, he is all-powerful, and without humility, destruction is inevitable. He is in charge of that small brood. His concern displays his meekness.

In the same way, God is "in charge, as always His eyes taking everything in, His eyelids unblinking, examining Adam's unruly brood" (Psalm 11:4 MSG). God's watchful care is a picture of his meekness, brokenness, and perseverance. He's humble because He chooses to be, not because He has to be. He can't be made to be humble, but to engage us without killing us, He bridles His all-consuming mightiness. This is so He can know us and empower us in the earth as representatives of greatness. That's why David said to the Father, "Your greatness has made me great" (Psalm 18:33 NKJV). Not His power but His greatness made him great.

He has also persevered at being the almighty God. He has never relinquished being God to anyone else. There is greatness to be had, and God is in charge of you having it, not the warlock, the witch, or the wizard. This is His world! He implemented the pie's principle. It is law. The pie has been and always will be determining your greatness!

WALK IN, BE CLOTHED WITH

We are told to walk with lowliness, gentleness, and long-suffering. This mandate was initially given almost two thousand years ago when the most common mode of transportation was walking. There were no trains, cars, or planes. They used camels, horses, and donkeys, but they utilized their feet as much as any of these animals. The carpenter to his shop, the farmer to his garden, and the shepherd to the fields. Walking was a necessary part of their lives. They walked all day long so when they were told to walk with lowliness, gentleness, and long-suffering, they understood that they were being asked to be lowly, gentle, and long-suffering all day long. Just like they had to have their feet produce for them to live, they would need the pie to reach their destiny.

This same line of reasoning applies to what the apostle Peter asked of us to "be clothed with humility" (1 Peter 5:5 NKJV). His audience was accustomed to wearing clothing that protected them from the scorching sun and sandstorms of Palestine. Everyone dressed in some form of protective apparel every day. They didn't have any synthetic fibers, personal fans, or sunblock. Instead, they had robes, dresses, and head wraps. The carpenter, the farmer, and the shepherd all dressed in their respected attire to protect their skin. Just as they had to have their clothes to protect their bodies, they would need humility to protect them from their own sun and sandstorm trials.

These instructions to "walk with and be clothed with humility" highlights another facet of humility, its elusive nature. There's no PhD in humbleness. It tends to escape the grasp of the greatest of Christians. It's the most elusive of all virtues. This is why a man can teach on humility one minute, and the next minute, that same man can be found in pride, violating the very principle he just taught on. You never arrive at a permanent place of humility. You must choose to walk in, to be clothed with this elusive virtue.

LIFE'S TOUGHEST DIGEST?

We have to be told to have such a commitment to humility because being humble is not natural for anyone. Some of us are quieter than others but not necessarily humbler. We are predisposed to being prideful. Humbleness is to say with John the Baptist, "He must become greater; I must become less" (John 3:30 NIV). God becomes greater through you as you "become less." Humbleness is resisting our prideful proclivities.

This resisting is counterintuitive to the highest law of man's nature, self-preservation. We are programmed with an innate desire to keep ourselves alive. It has helped us to survive. In itself, it is not bad, but unbalanced it produces self-absorption. Saint Paul echoed our inner drive to be self-made, saying that we are "self-absorbed, parents, crude, coarse, dog-eat-dog, unbending, slanderers, impulsively wild, savage, cynical, treacherous, ruthless, bloated windbags" (2 Timothy 3:2–4 MSG). Without the transformation that Christ gives, we treacherously, uncompromisingly seek to be self-made important people. Most people fail to deal with their animalistic instinct to be first and above all in some shape or fashion. We have inflated egos that constantly mislead us. We live as self-sufficient beings. That's why the pie is hard to stomach. It is life's toughest digest. It's the antithesis of the first instinct of man—keep himself and fabricate his own greatness. God designed us so well that we think we are adequate enough to run our own lives. He's the masterful designer.

Since self-preservation is the greatest universal law, not preserving yourself is the hardest thing in the universe to practice. This is because going against this law presents the greatest opposition in the universe to it—you. We absolutely are our own worst enemy. In the following chapters, we will explore more of the nature of humility, probe into its power, and discuss how to apply the many facets of the pie to our lives. Only humbleness can bring the needed balance to this law that has robbed so many of their significance, success, and satisfaction. The character, conduct, and contentment that God wants them to have. The scripture says, "Before his downfall, a man's heart is proud, but humility comes before honor" (Proverbs 18:12 NIV). Think back over your life. Everything you've failed at before you fell; your heat was proud first. Every time you've been honored, you had some of the pie first. Where you are in life now is a picture of this truth. It shows how much pie you have had. What will you schedule for your future? More downfalls because of today's pride or more honor because of today's pie?

A PIE AWAY

Let's go back to five hundred years ago where the kings were the privileged of the era. Being born into royalty, they would not so much as touch humble pie their entire life, but those disregarded organs were a staple in the common man's diet.

Interestingly enough, on average, the royal family didn't live any longer than the underlings they reigned over due to a filthy environment, poor hygiene, and antiquated medical care. The common folks lived just as long as the king and his family! Now a king was considered great because of his wealth and power. Yet his power, not his wealth, afforded him any more days on earth to enjoy his kingdom. In other words, the pie allowed the common man to share the greatness of the king in the form of days lived on God's beautiful earth. Those who were not born with a silver spoon in their mouth shared an aspect of greatness with royalty because humble pie levels the playing field. Kingly greatness is accessible to all. A royal life is within eating distance!

YOUR PIECE OF THE PIE:
A GREAT LIFE

So David went on and became great, and the
Lord God of host was with him.

—2 Samuel 5:10 (NKJV)

The Bible tells of God being glorified through normal people leading great lives. Its pages are filled with the stories of people with fruitful character, conduct, and contentment. They weren't perfect, but they were pie eaters. The great innovators, Adam and Eve. The great contractor, Noah. The great patriot, Father Abraham. The great mother, Sarah. The giant leader, Joseph. The great miracle worker, Moses. The great Councilman, Mordecai. The great governor, Nehemiah. The great warrior, David. They all bore glorious fruit.

You're supposed to be on that list too! That's why Saint Paul directs "whether you eat or drink or whatever you do, do all to the glory of God" (1 Corinthians 10:31 NKJV). That's not dining or working out while quoting some religious phrases. It's dining or working out without dishonoring the Father. When you do, heaven's list of greats enlarges.

King David was on that list. He "became greater and greater for the Lord god of hosts was with him" (Samuel 5:10 ESV). He didn't just arrive at destination greatness; he kept increasing among his peers. God increased his greatness and comforted him on every side because he increased the ways that he glorified God.

Like King David, you were born to increase in greatness. Refuse to let the narrative of your life end in any other way. Resolve to increasingly glorify God in every season of your life.

King David was a superb shepherd, prophet, musician, song composer, poet, inventor, and warrior. He kept contributing to the world around him at a high level. It was obvious that God was with him, soaking in increasing glory through the different hats that he wore. No matter what you do occupationally, socially, or for entertainment, do it honorably from heaven's perspective.

HIS PLAN FOR GREATNESS

The honorable King David lived close to God; he nurtured an organic relationship with Him. God said David was "a man after his own heart" (1 Samuel 13:14 NKJV). David's heart was calibrated to the heart of God. God "loves righteousness and justice" (Psalm 33:5 NKJV) and hates error. It's evil. David was known to "love the Lord" and "hate evil" (Psalms 97:10). Even though he messed up, he repented early and often.

The most accurate means of assessing our love for God is the sin that's in and around us, because our decisions display our love and hate interest. If I could view your texts, your Facebook page, your Instagram, or Snapchat feed, what would I find? God doesn't want to spoil your fun. He doesn't just think sin is a bad idea. He hates sin because it keeps you away from Him. It is counterproductive to His plan for your greatness.He would hate for you to miss out on a great life. That's essentially what sin (error) is—to miss out on the greatness that the Father has for you. Remember the first aspect of greatness—when God gets the most glory out of your life. To sin is to deny God glory, to dishonor Him. We've all done that. That's why the Bible says, "All have sinned and fall short of the glory of God" (Romans 3:23 NKJV). When God is not being glorified, we're missing the mark because it's all about the glory. "Glory to God in the church! Glory to God in the Messiah in Jesus! Glory down all the generations! Glory through all millennia! Oh yes!" (Ephesians 3:21 MSG). It's all about the glory!

IT'S THE STARTING POINT

Let's say you're single. You find a partner and decide to get married. You commit to spending the rest of your life in this monogamist relationship, endeavoring to please your spouse. Yet your spouse wants to see other people, drink every day, do drugs, party, and stay out all times of the night with their other partners. You wouldn't have a good relationship because of your different love and hate interest. Even if they decided to cut back, only cheat, drink, and do drugs on the weekends, you still wouldn't be close. You would be crushed, and a wall would erect between you two. You wouldn't give your spouse access to the greatness that a relationship with you provides.

It's the same with God; He is waiting to be committed to an intimate relationship with us, but it's our regular errors that keep him at Bay. They keep our relationship stale. We think we can still be close to Him because we cut back some of our cheating, but isn't some cheating still infidelity? He stays faithful, but our sins stifle our faith and our confidence in Him.

King David had confidence in God because for a while, it was true that he hated "every false way" (Psalm 119:104 NKJV). Everything that was fake, phony, cunning, and not of God, he detested. His heart was wherever God's heart was on all matters. However, God felt about sin, silver, statistics, and status he felt the same way. His relationship with God was the core reason for his great life. Everything else in his life was empowered to prosper because his heart was in tune with God's. A great relationship with God equals a God glorifying, impactful, and fulfilled life. One that'ssignificant because of selfless character,

- successful due to skillful conduct, and
- satisfied with soothing contentment.

Attention to this relationship is the starting point for the life God wants you to have. The only great life worth speaking of is the God life. It's the only one that lasts.

GOD'S SCHEMATICS

Wanting His disciples to have a walk with the Father, Jesus instructed them, "Embrace this God-life, and you will get God's everything" (Mark 11:24 MSG). God is wanting and waiting to dump His everything on men whose hearts are stuck on Him. In fact, "the eyes of the Lord run to and fro throughout the whole earth, to show Himself strong on behalf of those whose heart is loyal to Him" (2 Chronicles 16:9 NKJV). That is absolutely stunning! To know that God is seeking some calibrated hearts to show how mighty He is. He makes life's supposed losers win; they are loyal to Him. He is the advantage, and He is offering us His everything.It's true. "God is always on the alert, constantly on the lookout for people who are totally committed to Him" (2 Chronicles 16:9 MSG). He wants us to be great more than we want it for ourselves. He is not looking for the committed just to identify them. He wants to totally bless the totally committed. Greatness is His idea. It's His light for all of mankind. I don't know anybody who doesn't want that, a God who wants us to be remarkable and has the plan and power to make us remarkable. There is always going to be someone who's for you in life, but there help for you would be limited by their time, resources, and connections. Yet if God is for you, His help is efficacious. He's not limited by time, resources, or connections. He has all the time, all the resources, and all the connections you need.

He's yearning for the children of men to get serious about hosting Him, so His masterful life plans can be revealed. He says,

> I know what I am doing. I have it
> all planned out—plans to take care of
> you, not abandon you, plans to give you
> the future you hope for. When you call
> on me, when you come and pray to Me,
> I'll listen. When you come looking for
> Me, you'll find Me. Yes, when you get
> serious about finding Me and want it

more than anything else, I'll make sure you won't be disappointed. (Jeremiah 29:11–14 MSG)

The best plans available for your life are the original plans that your Maker has for you. His detailed schemes, methods, and arrangements are the ones that are tailor-made to "prosper you," not "harm you," and "give you hope and a future" (Jeremiah 29:11 NIV).

The only way to get God's schematics for your life though is to have a walk with Him. Regular fellowship with Him is what He charges for His masterful plans. The Bible spells it out, "Keep company with God, get in on the best" (Psalm 37:4 MSG). God has willingly obligated Himself forever to those who want His company, not the children who want to use Him for what He can do. He knows when our desire for Him is real and when it is not. You can't fake an interest in Him. You have to grow in your love with Him. Just as in any relationship, the more time you spend with Him, the more affectionate you become. He is capable of being known by all humans at all times simultaneously unveiling Hi plans for us all. But only the driven "get in on the best."

Be driven, intentional, one who preservers. "Don't look for shortcuts to God. The market is flooded with surefire, easy going formulas for a successful life that can be practiced in your spare time. Don't fall for that stuff, even though crowds of people do. The way to life—to God!—is vigorous and requires total attention" (Matthew 7:13–14). Your best life won't be awakened because you read one magazine or attended a seminar or purchase a surefire stock. Your best life will be awakened when you're willing to do these things regularly while vigorously attending to God.

OPPOSITION

Let me interject this truth; a great life will be opposed! The reason you have to be driven to God is because the enemy opposes greatness. In fact, your level of adversity in life is directly proportionate to your level of greatness in life. If it seems like all hell is coming against you, fences erecting at every turn, know that it's proportionate to your capacity for greatness. When the enemy is attacking you on a high level, it's because your ceiling for greatness is high.

King David was opposed by the most powerful man in the land, King Saul, because David contained the capacity to be a king himself. His opposition was evidence that his future was going to be bright. Great opposition is proof of a king's capacity because your level of adversity in life is directly proportionate to your level of greatness.

A king in his field, Saint Paul explained that "a great and effective door has opened to me, and there are many adversaries" (1 Corinthians16:9 NKJV). New opportunities were ahead of Saint Paul but so were the adversaries that were assigned to keep him out! Adversity is the signpost that identifies great and effective doors, new ways of doing things. Demonic activity is proof that you're in front of a new opportunity. Don't let resistance get you down. Get excited because the very presence of the enemy is evidence that you're at the threshold of a new season. If you respond correctly, humble yourself in opposition; it will be a mere prelude to your great life.

AN EXPERT

"This is God's message, the God who made earth, made it livable and lasting, known everywhere as God: 'Call to Me and I will answer you. I'll tell you marvelous and wondrous things that you could never figure out on your own'" (Jeremiah 33:2–3 MSG). He wants to tell us things that we wouldn't know otherwise. He wants to give us an edge in life. We just have to be close enough for the whisper of these "marvelous and wondrous things" that are outside of our database and understanding. He makes us privileged to information beyond our experience, expertise, and economics.

He's the only qualified expert worthy of guiding our lives. We've been led by others for too long. The Bible says, "Don't set people up as experts over your life, letting them tell you what to do. Save that authority for God; let Him tell you what to do. There is only one Life Leader for you" (Matthew 23:9–10). You should see what He has to say about everything. The world doesn't know who they are; they're faking it. Trust me. If their pillows could talk, they'd tell of the tears they cry at night because they don't have it all together. Paul reminds the Christians in Ephesus, "It wasn't so long ago that you were mired in that old stagnant life of sin. You let the world, which doesn't know the first thing about living, tell you how to live" (Ephesians 2:12 MSG). "Save that authority for God." Let God be your first consultant. Let Him dispel the fence of the unknown in your life. We let people who don't know what their purpose is tell us what ours should be. Said another way, we let people who aren't operating at greatness tell us what we can and cannot be great at. It's ignorant for us to listen to them. Yet this fence of ignorance doesn't have a chance when its opposing one that keeps company with God, the foremost expert on every subject and every field. That's exciting. The prophet Isaiah recognized His expertise, so he asked sarcastically, "Who could ever have told God what to do or taught Him His business? What expert would He have gone to for advice, what school would He attend to learn justice? What god do you suppose might have taught Him what He knows, showed Him how things work?" (Isaiah 40:13–14 MSG). God already has a working knowledge of every person, place, and thing on earth. They all exist within time, and He was here before the beginning of time. Time was His idea; thus, He's the expert on all things within it.

All technology has evolved under His watch. All people have matured with Him looking over them. Thus, if any device, system, or person is stopping you from experiencing the life God wants you to, you can consult Him directly. That's if you've paid the price to have His expertise. For example, you may be contemplating relocating for a job or marriage. Well, God knows where you would be the most efficient, influential, and fulfilled. You must first get all the natural information you can (what the educational system is, what your commute time will be, etc.). Then you'll need supernatural information, inner peace, to know what can't be known in the natural (what neighbors to stay away from, what church to attend, etc.). He knows about the people and positions that aren't in your life yet. He knows about the business, enterprises, and jobs that do not yet exist but will be featured in your future.

He's more than capable of giving us what we would call "the good life." He wants us to stick with Him during the good times and the bad so He can stay at work in us. Christians are "God's [own] handiwork (His workmanship) recreated in Christ Jesus, [born anew] that we may do those good works which God predestined [planned beforehand] for us [taking paths which He prepared ahead of time], that we should walk in them [living the good life which He prearranged and made ready for us to live]" (Ephesians 2:10 AMP). God's paths are prepared and awaiting the arrival of His kids. All other paths are inferior in regard to our significance, success, and satisfaction.

His paths are what His children have been "born anew" to discover and embrace. Parents have predetermined paths for their children to grow on. They ensure their protection, provision, and some pleasure in being alive. Yet even great guardians can't be as effective as possible if the child doesn't want to be close to them. The child would be willingly forfeiting much of the parents' wisdom, money, and influence that comes from intimacy with great guardians. Not being close to them would, to some degree, negate being born into a great family.

In the same way, God is a great Father. He is wiser than any earthly parent having foreordained paths for His children to grow on. He wants us to desire a deep, below-the-surface relationship with Him. We stop Him from being and doing all that He wants to be and do in our lives by our lack of fellowship with Him. He's waiting on us to come after Him. The Bible says, "Come close to God, and He will come close to you" (James 4:8 NLT). You don't have to forfeit any of God's wisdom, money, and influence because you haven't come close to Him. You can start drawing near to Him today.

He wants to protect, provide, and present a pleasurable life to His children—the ones who want His input in their daily lives. What's fascinating about God's fatherhood is that His children never become self-sufficient adults who don't need Him. His kids are forever "children of God" (Romans 8:16 NKJV). He doesn't have adults, nieces, nephews; He has children. That reality must be with you daily if a deep-rooted relationship is going to develop. Childlike dependency keeps the Father's pleasantness in route.

THE LIFE HE HAS

Having this type of dependency on the Father is not easy to maintain. If it was, the great life like King David had would be common. Everybody would have it, external success costs. You have to be willing to present your life to God to do what He pleases in your future. Knowing this, Saint Paul directs us, "Here's what I want you to do, God helping you: Take your everyday, ordinary life—your sleeping, eating, going to work, and walking around life—and place it before God as an offering. Embracing what God does for you is the best thing you can do for Him" (Romans 12:1 MSG). God wants to help us place our lives before Him as an offering, so He can give us all the help we need.

Compared to what God has done for us, offering our lives up to Him should be a no brainer. One of the greatest things I've learned about God that's exemplified in His word and history is that He always deals with us with our best interest at heart. He says, "I'm the Lord, and I do not change" (Malachi 3:6 NLT). He never has and never will deal with us in bitterness or selfish ambition. He is all-in for us. Who couldn't use this kind of care? He can do more with and for me than I could ever do for myself.

Jeremiah had this to say, "I know, God, that mere mortals can't run their own lives, that men and women don't have what it takes to take charge of life. So correct us, God, as You see best" (Jeremiah 10:23–24 MSG). To want God's best is to invite His constant correction. He's regularly issuing course corrections to have us in the proper place in life. None of us has what it takes to be our own pilots. There is too much that we know we don't know; then there is information that we don't know that we don't know that's affecting us. We are seriously handicapped without Him. Correct us as you see fit, Father God!King David needed a few course corrections during his life. At one point, he had committed adultery with Bathsheba, had her husband killed, and lied to cover it up. He completed a triple crown of evil from the most powerful seat in the land! How prideful he must have been. After he was confronted by the prophet Nathan, David swallowed his pride and, from a place of brokenness, cried, "God, make a fresh start in me, shape a Genesis week from the chaos of my life" (Psalm 51:10 MSG). David seen himself as the earth "without form and void" (Gen. 1:1 NKJV), needing the Creator's creativity and direction. He knew part of God's résumé was the first six days of creation. He created the universe, the sky, the earth, the sea, and every living thing that exist in them out of nothing. David had the right God for the task of fixing him.

He gave his life to God, so he could have the life God wanted him to have. He wasn't whole until he walked in God's path. He said, "God made my life complete when I placed all the pieces before Him. When I got my act together, He gave me a fresh start. Now I'm alert to God's ways" (Psalm 18:20 MSG). He was awakened to God's course for the remainder of his life. No matter where your life is now, if you give it to Him for keeping, He will "shape a Genesis week" from it. He will bring beauty out of confusion and chaos.

King David became great because he knew how to reconnect to the Father. He was able to help people and himself. We can do the same. The Bible directs us to "steep your life in God-reality, God-initiative, God provisions. Don't worry about missing out. You will find all your everyday human concerns will be met" (Matthew 6:33 MSG). When God is really first in our lives, when we prioritize and protect our relationship with Him, our everyday lives become His priority. We have to seek Him intentionally and genuinely to experience the "God reality."

Being steeped into the God-reality is having God as the centerpiece (focal point) of your life and not just the piece (focused on sometimes). Does your leisure time squeeze God out? What about your relationships? Even things that are good can compete with God when He's a piece and not the centerpiece.

A PIELESS LIFE, A GODLESS LIFE

God deserves to be the centerpiece of our life. It is evident that even though He didn't have to, He made us to be intimate with Him. We are the only part of His creation who can appreciate the rest of His creation. Plants and animals are not aware of their existence. He made us last so that we could enjoy Him and everything He made. But we can only enjoy Him and them through the same virtue that He deals with us through—humbleness the right estimation of self. God is always full of the pie so "we are not consumed" (Lamentations 3:22). The pie is present, so "God can't stomach arrogance or pretense; believe me He'll put those upstarts in their place" (Proverbs 16:5 NKJV). Arrogance and pretense cannot coexist with humbleness. They are mutually exclusive. Be assured that upstarts will be put in their place. God will see to it. Just keep watching; that movie ends the same way every time.

It can never be said that God is acting arrogantly or prideful. "Arrogance and pride-distinguishing marks in the wicked are just plain sin" (Proverbs 21:4 MSG). They are the distinguishing mark's in all that's evil and wrong in the world. God can't stand the smell of pride and pretense because they are sin. They act as repellents to your significance because they stop you from being close to Daddy God.

To be close to Him, you have to share His attitude toward pride. You must despise it. He is humble twenty-four hours a day, seven days a week. Therefore, if you're not into the pie, then you're not into Him. By default, you're into what He hates. You don't agree with God, "Can two walk together unless they are agreed?" (Amos 3:3 NKJV). A pieless life is a godless life!

"God opposes the proud, but favors the humble" (James 4:6 NLT). He's lined up against the pretentious know-it-alls, but He's assisting those who imitate Him. He's blocking some realms of greatness for the haughty and granting access to those same realms to the lowly.

Being arrogant repels God, being lowly attracts Him.

Ask the Apostle Paul. He was pridefully prosecuting God's movement and the earth. He was on his way to Damascus with permission from the high priest to arrest the Christians there. Damascus hosted a commercial network with trade reaching into Mesopotamia, Persia, and Arabia. If Christianity flourished in Damascus, it would reach those areas as well. The apostle thought he was doing what was right, but he was actually lined up against God. God knocked him off his beast to the ground as if to say, "Get off your high horse and sit in the dirt" (Isaiah 47:1 MSG). From that moment, he stopped persecuting the church and started promoting it. The apostle had an encounter with Jesus on Humble Drive that lined him up with the Father. You don't win when you line up against God; you get knocked down. Every time we are proud, we have chosen to be on the team opposing God. Even if you're doing a work for God, a proud attitude turns Him against you. You forfeit the blessing on your endeavors because you've got the wrong team jersey on.

Brother David had God's jersey on most of the time. At the core of his being, he had a shared interest with Him. They kept company because David learned the secret to companionship with God—humility. He wrote, "For though the Lord is on high, yet has He respect to the lowly [bringing them into fellowship with Him]; but the proud and haughty He knows and recognizes [only] at a distance" (Psalm 138:6 AMP). Humbleness is the prerequisite to fellowship with Him. He's not too busy to communicate with the pie eaters, but the proud doesn't get any of His time. Humility makes you desirable to Him because it makes room for His lordship. On his weekly broadcast, *World Impact*, I heard Dr. Billy Wilson say that "humility creates in us the greatest capacity to be intimate with God." It makes you fellowship compatible.

Doctor Wilson echoes what King David said of Him, "The high and lofty one who lives in eternity, the Holy One says this: 'I live in the high and holy place with those whose spirits are contrite and humble" (Isaiah 57:15 NLT). He's the highest and holiest being, and amazingly, He wants to accompany the humble around the earth. That's why he tells us to "listen and pay attention! Do not be arrogant, for the Lord has spoken" (Jeremiah 13:15 NLT). He is itching to have us next to his bosom, so he tells us how to qualify for His presence. Detach from arrogance and drive yourself to Him. Then be diplomatic enough to "listen and pay attention" to Him.

David listened and paid attention to God. He was the first king of Israel to be handpicked by God. When He chose a king for His people, it was a man in close covenant relationship with Him. A man who held that standing because he was broken, meek, and persistent. He was the greatest king in Israel's history. When Jesus came to earth, He was known as the "Son of David" (Matthew 9:27 NKJV). He was a man after God's "own heart" (1 Samuel 14:14 NKJV).

ARROGANCE—GOD'S DISPLEASURE

Since God invented time, it has been His desire for man, the apex of His inventions, to do as the Prophet Micah said, "Walk humbly with thy God" (Micah 6:8 KJV). Yet throughout history, it has been the lack of humility that we've mastered. Whenever our forefathers got off of Humble Drive, God was displeased. Adam and Eve left it deceived into thinking that God was withholding a better lifestyle from them. What pride, thinking they knew better than God.

Joseph's ten older brothers left Humility Avenue, being so jealous of him that they got into human trafficking selling him to the Ishmaelites. All because they didn't want their brother to be greater than them.

Pharaoh saw himself as a God demanding to be worshipped. He thought his Egyptian empire was indestructible, but his defeat came swiftly.

Samson had his own agenda for his life. Marrying whores, getting drunk, and getting a haircut were all forbidden by the Father. He was set aside as a child to be close to God, but in pride, he followed his own path to destruction.

King Saul was full of himself too. Having more power than anyone else in his kingdom didn't make him secure. He felt threatened when a young David was celebrated by some of his citizens. Since he was stuck on himself, he began to envy David. He even attempted to kill him several times. His lust for recognition tainted his perspective. The prophet Samuel told him, "When you were little in your own eyes, were you not the head of the tribes of Israel?" (1 Samuel 15:17 NKJV). When he ceased to be humble, he ceased to be great.

Nebuchadnezzar, the Babylonian King, is probably the best-known example of this arrogance. He had a dream of a large tree that grew very tall and strong. It was visible to many. It "had fresh green leaves, and it was loaded with fruit for all to eat" (Daniel 4:12 NLT). Wild animals found a home in its shade, and a host of birds nested in its branches. Then a messenger from heaven came down and commanded that the tree be cut down and the animals and birds be chased away but leave the stump and its root intact. This condition was to be for seven years.

None of the king's wise men could interpret it, so Daniel was called for. After hearing the dream, he knew exactly what it meant. "That tree, Your Majesty, is you. For you have grown strong and great; your greatness reaches up to heaven and your rule to the ends of the earth" (Daniel 4:22 NLT). It was true; Nebuchadnezzar resided over Babylon, the renowned city of its day. It was approximately fifteen square miles, protected by massive walls of over three hundred fifty feet high and over eighty feet thick. It was strategically positioned with a river running it. The fruit and vegetables produced were enough to feed more than one million citizens. It was a masterful metropolis. Earthly speaking, King Nebuchadnezzar was great, but he glorified himself, which limited his impact, and gave him a fleeting sense of fulfillment. Daniel continued, "You'll be driven from human society, and you will live in the fields with the wild animals. You will eat grass like a cow, and you will be drenched with the dew of heaven" (Daniel 4:25 NLT). Talk about being humbled, going from the palace to the plains. Daniel let him know that it was his pride that was causing this and schooled him. "You will live this way until you learn that the Most High ruled over the kingdoms of the world and gives them to anyone he chooses" (Daniel 4:25 NLT). He was to learn the lesson of the ages.

Sure enough, one day, he was taking a walk on the flat roof of his royal palace in Babylon. As he looked out across the city, he said, "Look at this great city of Babylon! By my own mighty power, I have built this beautiful city" (Daniel 4:30 NLT). While he was stroking his ego against God's grain, God humbled him, bringing Daniel's interpretation to pass. He was "driven from human society" (Daniel 4:32 NLT). He lived in the fields with the wild animals and ate grass like a cow. "His hair was as long as eagle's feathers, and his nails were like bird's claws" (Daniel 4:33 NLT). The medical term for this condition is called lycanthropy. It is when a human acts like a lycanthrope (a werewolf). He had temporarily lost his mind.

His condition lasted for seven long years until one day in a moment of clarity, he came to himself. God touched his mind, and he started praising and worshiping the Lord God, saying, "His role is everlasting, and His kingdom is eternal" (Daniel 4:34 NLT). He went on to confess his wrong, "Now I, Nebuchadnezzar, praise and glorify and honor the King of heaven. All His acts are just and true, and He is able to humble the proud" (Daniel 4:37 NLT). He knew that it was his pride that was to blame for his situation.

Look at the root of your condition. Is there a proud scene to blame? You may not say what the King said, but do you share his attitude? Do you give yourself the glory for what you have or what you can do? Don't wait for seven years of lost to find yourself. Recognize His eternal rule while you still can. Don't wait until your life is scary like a werewolf to glorify God.

Nebuchadnezzar wouldn't humble himself; God had to do it for him. He set him right on Humble Drive. The beautiful thing about having your ego broken is that you're positioned to recognize God and be recognized by Him. Remember, "humility creates in you the greatest capacity to be intimate with God." It's drawing the Great One to you, bringing greatness out of you.

COMMAS AND SEMICOLONS

Adam and Eve, Joseph's brothers, Pharaoh, Samson, King Saul, and King Nebuchadnezzar could have chosen the pie. It was their pride that kept them from knowing God intimately, and not knowing Him intimately kept them from being great in that season. They wrote their own stories, starring themselves, and costarring God.

I want to let the world in on what Jesus is asking us all, "Do you have any idea how silly you look writing a life story that's wrong from start to finish, nitpicking over commas and semicolons" (Matthew 23:24). When God is not first in your life (when you're not getting His help), you are living a life that He has not authorized. Without proximity to Him, you will not have the assistance that He wants to give, and in irritation, you will be "nitpicking over commas and semicolons," insignificant things in your life. Wrong focus breeds aggravation. But to be in sync with God is to say with Jesus, "The father is the goal and the purpose of life" (John 14:28 MSG). He relieves us of our nitpicking.

When the pie is digested, your capacity to contain greatness enlarges. Minor things won't bother you as much. Frivolous matters won't worry you; they stay in their place. Your job performance will increase, and your relationships will be refreshed. Make Him the goal and purpose of your life, and you will have eternal success. Every comma and semicolon will fall in place.

A LIFE OF PRAYER

What does the Father being the goal of your life look like? We speak of being close to God, whom we can't see, so it's subjective language. In other words, my relationship with God may look different than yours, but if our hearts were examined, you will find my Jesus reigning supreme. You know He's been made the goal of your life when

His perspective, His power, and His presence are elevated above yours.

Now this relationship with God is a spiritual one. It's intangible, but it has tangible manifestations like prayer. We must repent in prayer often. If you can look back at a time that you were closer to God than you are now, then you backslid to get there. Repent. Or if you've never known him, repent for living on your own and accept his schematics for your life, starting with salvation. This is further explained in chapter 11.

Josiah, king of Judah, repented. He accepted God's schematics for his life. His high priest, Hildah, informed him that he hadn't been pleasing the Lord. He wasn't keeping God's law, so God wasn't happy with him or his subjects. Judgment was coming. Immediately, King Josiah took a slice of the path. What a life lesson! When judgement is impending, get to Humble Drive first. No matter what the fence is (money, relational troubles, or the like), train yourself to get low first. Let your response come from there. There the king repented and prayed, and God spoke through the interpreter Hildah. "Because your heart was tender, and you humbled yourself before God when you heard His words against this place and against its inhabitants, you tore your clothes before me, I also have heard you said the Lord" (2 Chronicles 34:27 NKJV).

The king went after God in brokenness. God smelled its sweet aroma and hearkened unto Josiah's voice. Humility drew a response from God. It serves as a magnet for the voice of God. The pie is a microphone that amplifies the auditorium of heaven where God releases His wisdom. He's speaking words of peace, affirmation, and knowledge, but only the persistent, meek, and broken are hearing His "gentle and quiet whisper" (1 Kings 19:12 MSG). Who are you more like King Josiah or King Nebuchadnezzar?

The king you resemble will be determined by the company you keep. Show me your company, and I'll tell you if you're more like King Josiah (quick to the pie) or King Nebuchadnezzar (forced to the pie).

I was in prayer one day for an old ministry friend Bro Thomas, whom I hadn't seen or heard from in some ten years or so. I heard the Lord say that it was time for him to do what was in his heart concerning ministry and he was to take his home church (that he was not the pastor of) to the next level. It wasn't spooky; there was no rushing wind or lightning from heaven. God often speaks through interruptions in our own thoughts or heart impressions. He lives inside of us. He speaks through our faculties; it often sounds like yourself. I had heard from on high concerning Thomas's situation, and I wanted to share it with him, but I didn't have a phone number, an e-mail, or snail mail address to contact him. Yet I knew that if this was God, this word would reach him. I simply prayed, "God, you have to make this happen."

The following day, I called my brother-in-law who just so happened to be driving to the church where Brother Thomas was guest speaking. I told my brother-in-law what the Lord had put on my heart. Once he arrived, he was able to get Brother Thomas to his cell phone. I shared with him the word that I thought was just a general word of encouragement. To my surprise, he began to cry. He proceeded to tell me that just a week earlier, he had shared this sentiment with his wife in prayer (it's time to do what's in my heart concerning ministry), and that there was no way that I could have known that. He said I had confirmed a lot of things. Only God knew that a week later he would meet with his senior pastor to schedule his ordination for public ministry, something he had struggled with accepting for years.

He was on the mind of God; I just got close enough to listen in. It was a part of His plan for both of our lives—for me to speak and him to hear. My first conversation with him in almost a decade.

The auditorium of heaven is releasing words for the sons of God so that we might live at an advantage in this troubled world. He is telling us what to invest in, what relationships to choose, and what career to master. He even wants to give us peace about what car to buy and what home to live in. I often ask Him questions and wait to gauge the peace that I have in that moment. Saint Paul declared, "Let the peace (soul harmony which comes) from Christ rule (act as umpire continually) in your hearts" (Colossians 3:15 AMP). An umpire cannot be neutral. His job is to make a call. The baseball player is in or he is out; he's safe or he's not. Our great umpire, God, doesn't want to confuse us. He wants us to keep believing Him to guide us continually with His calls of peace. Persevere, my friend. Return to your prayer closet, repenting often to receive your marching orders.

When true prayer takes place (speaking and listening), the will of God is put into action. That's what prayer is—releasing the heart of God into the earth. It's when you say what God wants to be said down here. He puts desires into our hearts, then because of our dominion in the earth, we speak His desires into existence. It's why King David instructs us to "delight yourself also in the Lord, and He shall give you the desires of your heart" (Psalm 37:4 NKJV). He brings the desires to pass that He puts there. People will be encouraged, strengthened, and transformed to the glory of God. God put a desire in Brother Thomas's heart, then He opened up the door so I could share it with him.

SCHEDULE IT

Prayer will also increase your desire to model His character. This is strengthened by staying aware of the fact that you've been given a fresh start, "created new. The old life is gone; a new life burgeons! Look at it! All this comes from the God who settled the relationship between us and Him" (2 Corinthians 5:17–18 MSG). Greatness is possible because the great God's settlement made Him accessible. Remind yourself of this while you're in the grocery store, the drive-through, on your way to work, school, the mall, everywhere you go. That connects you with Him. Reconnecting has to be a daily goal. The humble know they need to reconnect in prayer daily to sustain godly character.

You are going to be bombarded with all kinds of reasons not to pray. Your mind will resist praying, but resolve to let your mind exhaust itself, then begin your prayer. Have some place in your home where you meet with Him daily. Schedule it. When something is important to us, it can be found on our schedule. As the old saying goes, "Schedule it, lest you neglect it." It's not a waste of time to commune with Him, to have Him permanently penciled in. Bathe in His love for you. Pray to Him. Worship Him quietly and with singing. Listen to Him. Check in with Him hourly acknowledging His presence.

My friend, Minister Vernon Ripley, has one of those watches that beeps at the top of every hour. No matter where he's at or what he's doing at that time, he stops and silently checks in with the Father. Any concerns or praise reports that arose in the previous hour are given to Him then. That's an awesome reminder to love on our eternal, invisible Father. Every hour, we can wait silently for His desires to invade our pursuits.

I'm calling believers to see God the way we do oxygen. We inhale it, and it takes life throughout our bodies. We should feel that if we don't breathe Him in, we can't make it. He can't just be like washing your car, you get around to Him on the weekends. That approach to God will get you weekend remnants of a great life, but if you depend on Him the way you do your next breath, He will bring greatness to every area of your life.

CAUTION

I'm not advocating developing a legalistic prayer life, one that you feel condemned if you miss a session. No. The Christian's relationship with God is secure because of Jesus. We pray, study, and live for Him because we get to be in covenant with Him. It doesn't matter if you miss a week of praying. You shouldn't, but if you do, you aren't going to hell. Your senses will be dull though because relationally you are drifting away from Him. Evil won't bother you as much, and you will be more prone to sin. You will conform to the world. Positionally you'll be in good standing with God. You're still righteous and holy, but conditionally you'll embrace unrighteousness (things that aren't right). So don't feel condemned while developing your prayer life but be aware of the greatness that you are leaving on the table.

You can start with ten minutes a day. Don't bite off more than you can chew but be committed to what you do bite off. It will increase in time. Whoever you spend time with, your affection for them will grow.

INTIMACY

Our prayer life is essential to being intimate with God. That is the goal of the most significant people on earth. It is God's greatest priority for our lives. Dr. Charles Stanley shares this sentiment in his book, *30 Life Principles*. His first principle sums up this chapter. "Intimacy with God—His highest priority for our lives—determines the impact of our lives." He wants us to be successful and satisfied, but above all else He wants us to be close to Him. So if you have to lose your kingdom, the place where you reign to find Him like King Nebuchadnezzar, He will let it happen. He wants your communion more than He wants you to be comfortable. He's waiting to shape a Genesis week out of your life, so you can change the world. The degree to which you're intimate with God is the same degree that you will be impactful. I want to be as close to God, the Impactor, as I can be. The Bible says of King Uzziah, "As long as he sought the Lord, God made him prosper" (2 Chronicles 26:5 NKJV). As long as he made intimacy with God a priority, God made it His priority to prosper him, to give him His everything. The king wanted to be close to the Impactor, Father God. Do you? He was driven to God, that is persistent in his pursuit of Him.

*P*ersistence

*I*gnites

*E*xcellence

The excellence of prosperity was ignited because he sought the Lord. God made him greater and greater because he got to God.

YOUR PIECE OF THE PIE:
A GREAT CAREER

For Mordecai was great in the King's palace, and his fame
spread throughout the provinces; for this man Mordecai
became Increasingly prominent.

—Esther 9:4 (NKJV)

I was one of three kids who was fine playing by myself. I spent a lot of time alone in my backyard and in the woods directly behind the yard. The funny thing about my time alone back then was about what I was doing. I was preaching to my imaginary congregation with all the gestures and voice inflections that I had witnessed at church. The birds would hear of being in the world, but not of the world. The worms were given a call to repentance. I saw myself as a pastor. Not only would I preach, but I would organize my make-believe congregants and dish out orders to my beloved deacon board.

I was raised in the church. My father is a pastor, and his father was a pastor. It was as if I was choosing to preach based on what I had been exposed to, but more accurately, it was choosing me. A lot of people overlook what they could be doing simply because they're familiar with it, whether it be cooking, cleaning, writing, managing, or just being hospitable. A business could be built around them all, a great career can be had.

A GREAT OCCUPATION

A great career can be defined as having a great job, being able to explain your work, being better than average, excelling in your practices, and regularly creating new systems, styles, and forms of service so the maximum amount of people can benefit, and the least mount be sorrowed of service.

That's what our Israelite brother, Mordechai, had. He was the chief executive to King Ahasuerus. Having that position, all the king's servants within the city gates were commanded to bow and pay homage to him. He had the king's signet ring with which He could purchase anything in the land. He could send out decrees with the king's authority because he was second-in-command in the land. His work clothes were "royal apparel of blue and white, with a great crown of gold and a garment of fine linen and purple; and the city of Shushan rejoiced and was glad" (Esther 8:15 NKJV). He had a great job, and the people were better off because of it. He was a great fit for his great occupation.

His responsibilities were to advise the king, conduct business transactions, and pronounce judgments on the king's behalf. He also demanded the respect of all the government officials. "For Mordecai was great and the King's palace, and his fame spread throughout all the providences; for this man Mordecai became increasingly prominent" (Esther 9:4). It's clear that he made the right career choice, one that used his gift of administration and allowed him to advance and grow. It also connected him to the people who needed him the most. Our problem is that we spend too much time on jobs that don't allow us to serve others with the gifts and talents that God has given us.

A great career is one that lets you express your gifts, talents, and competence. It provides you an opportunity to advance and is not a dead-end job. It allows you to grow as a person because of your interactions with people who you're required to help. Also, a great career will meet your financial needs or allow you the time to meet them.

God is not against His kids having career success. Most of the children of God are not mega church pastors. They work nine to five. Dr. Mark Chironna says that only 15 percent of Christians are in full-time ministry, the other 85 percent are in the marketplace. The Lord wants us to prosper in all our endeavors. He's not looking for anymore monks. He wants representatives in every field. A voice in astronomy, mechanics, engineering, computers, manufacturing, entertainment, government, education, etc. He wants us to "go into all the world" (Mark 16:15 NKJV). That is geographically and occupationally. The world of North and South America, Europe, and Australia (geographically), then the world of banking, the world of sports, the world of science and technology (occupational).

GREAT RELATIONSHIPS

To have a great career is to have great relationships. It's to be preferred by the right associates. The journey to a thriving career is paved with them. Ask anyone you deem successful about their career, and they'll tell you that they had help. There's always one or two connections that makes success possible; someone behind the scenes opens doors for you that would otherwise remain closed. In an interview with Pastor Benny Hinn in 2013, Rabbi Daniel Lapin said, "To be more successful, you have to be known by more people, be liked by more people, and be respected by more." Being known, liked, and respected by more people deals you a net of potential relationships for the connections you'll need in the future seasons of your life.

Great relationships do just that. They connect you to the next season. They don't constantly drain you; they upgrade you. There are deposits and withdrawals in them, but not disappointments or abuse. No one needs to feel that they are being taken advantage of. God uses people to bless our careers.

It was the great relationship that Brother Mordecai had with his younger cousin, Queen Esther, that took his career to a new height. Before Mordecai became great in the king's palace, Haman, the evil opponent of the Jews, was King Ahasuerus's chief advisor. After a failed attempt of slaughtering the Jews (Mordecai's family), King Ahasuerus had Haman put to death. He was hung on the very gallows that in his unjustified hatred, he had prepared for Mordecai. Then on that day, King Ahasuerus "gave Queen Esther the estate of Haman, the archenemy of the Jews. And Mordecai came before the king because Esther had explained their relationship. The King took off his signet ring, which he had taken back from Haman, and gave it to Mordecai. Queen Esther appointed Mordecai over Haman's estate" (Esther 8:1–2 msg). His relationship with Queen Esther landed him a promotion that included being responsible for the estate of his archenemy!Mordecai had power. If he wanted to implement a law, all he had to do was write it and seal it with his ring. When he spoke, things happened. Yet without Queen Esther, he would've been admiring the king from afar. Though he had a great mind, great faith, great vision, and great power, the door for that promotion had to be opened from the inside. He was qualified, but it was his great relationship with Queen Esther that linked him to his exalted position.

Dr. Michael Murdock is famous for saying, "When Satan wants to curse you, he sends a person into your life. But when God wants to bless you, He sends a person into your life." You're not ten years away from the next season of your life; you're one person away from the next season of your life. Somebody is exceling at the right thing, at the right place, and at the right time. That's the right person set to move into your life to further your career. In Mordecai's case, it was his younger cousin. It may be a relative, a coworker, a church member, an old associate, or it may be someone who doesn't know you exist yet. Whoever it is, the right relationship will bless your life.

I recently heard on a CNN program that the average American will change their career five times before they die. That's five different positions with five organizations and probably at five different pay rates. In most cases, changing careers is essentially starting over. A great relationship can serve as a link to your next career and make that transition as smooth as possible. Never underestimate the power of an inside man (an influential voice) designed to swing the pendulum in your direction.

I pray that the Lord would move on the hearts of influences. I pray that new doors of opportunity be opened to you in Jesus's name!

DEMAND

Another aspect of a great relationship is it is often demanding. Time, for instance, is often required to discover, develop, and deepen connections. Christians should speak to everyone we see every day. I know everyone doesn't have an outgoing, courageous personality, but we can all be warm and receptive. This gives God more to use. Speaking communicates availability. Tomorrow morning, just go throughout the factory or the office and greet all of your fellow employees and bosses. Sow those seeds of pleasantness, and in time, you will discover some new alliances.

Developing relationships takes time. For most people, a text here and there or a follow or like on social media will suffice if you don't see them regularly. But significant relationships take more time, energy, and effort to maintain. Texts, calls, and cards are good means of keeping in touch to maintain, but development requires more. For example, "Everyday Mordecai strolled beside the court of Haran to find out how Queen Esther was and get news of what she was doing" (Esther 2:11 MSG). A perfect gentleman, Mordecai was investing in the right relationship.

Deepening, enriching, and strengthening a relationship will require time as well. It requires the enlarging of trust. Before Esther was queen, she spent twelve months in the king's harem, preparing herself with beauty treatments. "Six month's treatment with oil and myrrh followed by six months without perfumes and various cosmetics" (Esther 2:12 MSG). She was gaining the king's trust. She wanted to be known, liked, and trusted by him.

Then look at Esther's relationship with Mordecai. Because of anti-Semitism, he commanded her not to say anything to him because she trusted him. Far from the surface, they shared a deep friendship. Their friendship illustrates how a great relationship can put demands on your potential. As the king's chief adviser, demands would be placed on Mordecai. Queen Esther got him the position, but his understanding, wisdom, and discernment would keep him there. This was the highest, best-paying position he had ever had. All would know shortly if he had the ability to excel in that position or not because of all the kingly issues that would be on his plate. You have to be squeezed sometimes to know how much endurance, ability, and patience you have.

Mordecai put demands on Ester's queenly abilities too. He had a large request for her. She was to deny her culture's diet, clothes, entertainment, and history. Her Jewish heritage was to be ignored. Mordecai didn't know for sure if Esther was mature enough to carry out his order, for she had never been asked to do anything like that before. Her potential as a queen was being leaned on. The demands deepened the relationship between them.

IT'S TWO-SIDED

See how great relationships have a give and take? Mordecai, and Esther pushed each other to be greater. Greater than the other potential queens, and greater than the other councilmen to the king. Greater relationships go both ways. When they don't, one side begins to feel used, and eventually resentful. No association can survive regular withdrawals by one party and no deposits. It's natural to take what we can get or to make all the relational withdrawals. Yes, it takes character to reciprocate deposits. It also takes acts of kindness to go further in displaying what Jesus said to "do to others as you would have them to do unto you" (Luke 6:31 NLT).

Since we're all flawed, we all offend each other. The nature of the relationship determines how frequent offenses come. Whether it's your employer, counselor, or family member, offenses cripple the discovery, development, and deepening of relationships. We can't let our flaws nor the flaws of others stop us from having something great that would benefit the kingdom. Be driven to discover great relationships, diplomatic in developing them, and detached from offenses in deepening them.

THE DIET

How can I acquire, cultivate, and strengthen these relationships? The pie. The dish that's most often left on the table because we don't like to be thought of as weak or ignorant. We like having all the answers.

Mordecai had some answers. The Bible sings some high praises of him. "The account of the greatness of Mordecai, to which the king advanced him, are they not written in the book of the Chronicles of the kings of Media and Persia? For Mordecai the Jew was second to King Ahasuerus, and was great among the Jews and well received by the multitude of his brethren" (Esther 10:2–3 NKJV). His position afforded him the opportunity to have a lasting impact. We should desire better positions so we can have positive effects on others for the glory of God. Mordecai's noble actions put him in the history books. He found the balance of being the second most powerful man in the land professionally and being liked by his peers. When a lot of the right people like you, you know you are doing something right. Mordecai didn't just wake up one day as this popular vice president of Persia—a lot of hard work went into his personal development, his family, and his career. Work that requires the perseverance, meekness, and brokenness of the pie. He was driven to God, diplomatic with people, and detached from offending both God and people.

When we're first introduced to him in the Bible, he's taking a slice of the pie. After the death of Esther's parents, Mordecai willingly "adopted her" (Esther 2:7 MSG). He was her older cousin, but he wasn't obligated to take her in. Yet from Brokenness Boulevard, he would pour hours of care, concern, and correction into her. You are positioned for a promotion when you willingly take on responsibility that you could let pass you by. He could have let Esther remain an orphan, but he had the meekness to know that he could strike the balance between working and parenting. He was broken enough to be an inexperienced first-time parent.

BE AWARE

We're told that he "was an attendant in the king's court" (Esther 2:11 AMP). He was a lowly servant, so low-key that King Ahasuerus didn't even know he was on his staff. He solved problems behind the scenes, including a plan to assassinate the king. When he heard of the King's danger, he notified Queen Esther, and the king was saved. Mordecai just so happened to uncover this conspiracy because he was accustomed to "sitting at the King's gate" (Esther 2:9 MSG). The king's gate was where prominent business and legal transactions took place. He was where things were happening.

If you want what he had, you have to be persistent enough to stay around information. You're not too old to be an intern at a corporation you would like to be employed by. You are not too busy to ask questions at a courthouse, a mechanic's shop, a church, or where you're currently employed. There's a hot spot where God wants to make you privileged to some information beyond your experience, your expertise, and your economics. Like Mordecai, you have to get in your field's hot spots.

Mordecai didn't hesitate to inform Queen Esther of the plot. He didn't care about what the other attendants thought of him. Today, some people call giving information to a superior "telling." There's a cultural disdain for it as if you're being disloyal to your coworkers. I know no one likes a tattletale. But we learn from Mordecai to do good regardless of the naysayers. You become valuable to others when you have the integrity to do the right thing when not doing it would be easier. God will honor it. Good deeds are seeds sown that will bring forth a harvest of future success.

BE AVAILABLE

We learn from Mordecai's example that we should be available.

Be available to our family, employers, coworkers, and if we have them, employees. Mordecai learned of the plan to take out the king, then he made it available to the queen. She could count on him. He was her go-to guy. Be the go-to guy in your department. Be knowledgeable, reliable, and trustworthy. Stay faithful and you will be recognized. In those days, Mordecai was at the king's gate every day. He didn't uncover an assassination plot every day, but he kept returning, working, and listening. Are you humble enough to make yourself accessible daily? Your recognition, a raise, a promotion, or a bonus will come.

BE ACTIVE
MAKING SOMETHING HAPPEN

Finally, Mordecai teaches us to make something happen. If there's no attractable activity, then manufacture some. By taking the information that he was made aware of to the queen, Mordecai saved the king's life. His actions became the talk of the town. It was recorded in the king's record book. Later when this matter was read to the king, he gave Mordecai an extravagant bonus. He ordered that he be paraded around in royal apparel so the kingdom would see how the king treats one in whom he wants to honor. Do you do anything that makes your workplace interesting? Are people curious about your occupation? Are you the one who makes something happen?

If you do these three things that Mordecai did, you will have a great career:

1. Be aware
2. Be available
3. Be active

A BONUS

The king went about honoring Mordecai as unique. After he was made aware of Mordecai's act of loyalty, he asked his servants if there was anyone in the courtyard. His then Chief Advisor Haman, just so happened to be out there wanting to speak with him. The king sent for him and asked Haman, "What would be appropriate for the man the King especially wants to honor?" (Esther 6:6 MSG). It's funny because in his pride, Haman thought the king was wanting to honor him. The proud are always consumed with themselves. He wanted some of the king's clothes and one of the royal horses to be paraded around in to display his power, so he suggested some royal clothes and a royal ride. To his surprise, the king then ordered him to bestow this honor, leaving nothing out upon the man he despised, Mordecai. Evidence that God can use your enemies to bless you. God can use people who don't even like you to bless you.

A bonus or a promotion could come from as association that you have yet to discover, develop, or deepen. In Mordecai's case, God made a racist (Haman) not only bless him but choose the blessing that he wanted for himself! Stop trying to figure out how God is going to bless you. He wants us to be blessed by staying aware that "promotion cometh neither from the east, nor from the west, nor from the south, but God is the judge: He putteth down one, and setteth up another" (Psalm 75:6,7 KJV). God controls, the marketplace moves.

A STUDIOUS ANSWER

Mordecai was exceptional at getting along with people. As a low-ly servant in the king's court, he talked to different people every day. People were comfortable conversing with and around him. He was a listener, and he was listened to because he had wise things to say. You want to be known not for playing all the time (there's nothing wrong with fun in moderation), not for being a prune that never has fun but for being wise, balanced, and meek.

The Bible gives us the secret to cultivating this meekness. It says, "The heart of the righteous studies how to answer" (Proverbs 15:28 NKJV). The believer is to be humble enough to learn about other people to increase their EQ (emotional intelligence) in order to be an effective servant in the home, church, and career.

LEARN NAMES

One thing to study to answer people with is their names. We have to put forth the necessary effort to learn people's names. There's nothing more professional than knowing the names of those around you. We like to hear our name called because it distinguishes us from others. Favor may be awakened all because you got a name right. When you need to get someone's attention, start with the most pleasant sound to their ears, what they have answered to since they were born. Study it, don't mispronounce it, and don't shorten it unless you have permission. When I hear my name, I instantly know two things: (1) that you know enough about me to distinguish me from others; and (2) you respect me enough to use that distention. That's the greatest start available since most people are thinking about themselves all the time anyway. Calling that name means you're thinking about them too.

HONOR OTHERS

Another thing to study before you've regularly answered others is how to communicate with honor. That is, with love and respect. People are to be valued. We must honor greatness in others no matter how insignificant or grand it may be. Always value people enough to communicate their worth in all conversations. This ensures the best possible outcome.

Give people your undivided attention. Treat them all like they're the most important person in the world. It doesn't matter if it's a business negotiation, a work transaction, or a family interaction. Saint Paul said it like this, "Make the most of every opportunity. Be gracious in your speech. The goal is to bring out the best in others in a conversation, not put them down, not cut them out" (Colossians 4:5–6 MSG). It requires a conscious decision to resist the urge to have uncivilized conversations. It's easy to be rude, condescending, and patronizing, but to honor all is normal from the waitress to the taxi driver, to the evil boss or employee. Everyone has something they can be complimented for (hard work, politeness, professionalism, a nice shirt, or a neat haircut). Be gracious. It will assist you in maximizing every opportunity and bringing the best out of others, the best response, the best decision, and the best effort. People thrive on the fuel of honor.

Honor people's office and personal space. Take interest in them as represented by their personal pictures, paintings, artifacts, and furniture. Comment on things that are unique about the individual and their space. Don't pry, don't be pushy or overbearing, and don't attempt to go where they don't invite you. Honor the distance that they choose to keep. Be ever aware. The humble are always reading the situation, quietly gauging all interactions.

LEARNING PERSONALITIES

In addition to learning names and communicating with honor, you must also study people's personalities. A person's personality is how they are prone to answer and react. It's their general emotional, mental, and behavior traits. Made popular in the 1980s are the four personality types. The sanguine (wants to have fun), the phlegmatic (wants peace), the choleric (wants control), and the melancholy (wants perfection). Everyone has a primary personality type and probably a mixture of some of the other personality traits as well.

An individual's personality matters because it determines how they process information and what they will do with it, if anything at all. For example, let's say you have an idea that will make your company a sizeable profit. Let's say your boss is a sanguine. You will want to bring the idea to him or her in an effective possibly entertaining way while keeping the atmosphere light. Get him smiling, and you've made a connection. If your boss is a phlegmatic, then you'll want to present it to him in a nonconfrontational way. Highlight your ideal solution to the existing conflict, and he'll want to know more. If your boss is a choleric, then you'll want to present it to him as if it's his own idea. Since he seeks to regulate everything, you may have to hint around your idea and lead him to it. When he comes to the conclusion you desired, he'll probably take credit for it, but at least your idea will be carried out. If your boss is a melancholy, then you'll want to bring it to him in an organized manner making sure you have all the numbers and relevant details. He'll appreciate the time and work you put into your presentation.

In dealing with people, I try to take my time taking the lowly road, deciphering my acquaintance's attitude. I'm studying to answer their primary personality type. I'm aware that I'm a sanguine, and as such, I'm prone to make decisions quickly so I can move on to the next one. Phlegmatics tend to make decisions to please as many people as possible in order to minimize contentions. Cholerics, who are natural leaders, tend to make decisions for everybody and will manipulate situations so they can have control. Melancholies are predisposed to making decisions that will display order so that everyone and everything is perfectly in place. Knowing our personality type—not who we've been conditioned to be by our culture or childhood but knowing our natural personality type—allows us to maximize our strengths and minimize our weaknesses. Then we'll benefit the maximum amount of people and sorrow the minimum amount of people. A lot of offenses can be mended or avoided all together if we take the time to see how people are programmed to respond.

Our personalities mix differently. There will be rough times, but we must continue to pursue people. Saint Paul said, "I don't want any of you sitting around on your hands. I don't want anyone strolling off down some path that goes nowhere. And mark that you do this with humility and discipline—not in fits and starts, but steadily, pouring yourselves out for each other in acts of love, alert at noticing differences, and quick at mending fences" (Ephesians 4:1 MSG). The Father doesn't want us to be passive in regard to relationships. He wants us to humbly give ourselves unto others with the following: "Acts of love"—learning names

1. Being "alert at noticing differences"—learning to honor others
2. "Quick at mending fences"—learning personality types

Studying to answer is the answer to the question, "How /can you/ discover, develop, and deepen great relationships?"

BE FRIENDLY

God made us to be different individuals with varying needs. That's why we must treat everyone as if they're the most important person in the world. Because at that moment, they should be. That's what honoring them is—treating them importantly.

It is true that you never know who you're going to need. Our needs are different because of our varying level of exposure, experience, and education. Our needs are met differently because of the four personality types. We need the pie so we'll be willing to identify and meet the needs around us.

God wants His representatives to be friendly, not stuck on themselves. We're commanded to "get along with each other, don't be stuck up. Make friends with nobodies, don't be the great somebody" (Philippians 2:16 MSG). Christians are to be polite always and accessible often to people we deem unworthy of our time. We are to constantly scatter seeds of friendliness. How do you treat your Uber (or taxi) driver, your cashier, your waitress, your garbage collector? How do you treat people who make less money than you do?

The fruit of God's spirit in us is friendly. They're relational values "things like affection for others, exuberance about life, serenity. We develop a willingness to stick with things, a sense of compassion in the heart, and a conviction that a basic holiness permeates things and people. We find ourselves involved in loyal commitments, not needing to force our way in life, able to marshal and direct our energies wisely" (Galatians 5:22–23 MSG). That is optimal fruit. When we're producing it then, we're honoring the Father by representing Him being the best expression of ourselves.

HUMILITY AND HUMOR

One of the indicators that you're being the best expression of yourself is your willingness to laugh. Are you predisposed to laughing? The Bible says, "A cheerful disposition is good for your health; gloom and doom leave you bone tired" (Proverbs 17:22 MSG). Laughter makes you and your environment healthy, but gloom and doom suck the life out of you and everything you're a part of. Choose to be optimistic to kill pessimism and cynicism. When a bad report comes in, frame it into the big scheme of things and choose to find the humor in it. People like to be around merriness. That's one of reasons great believers crave the presence of God. He is jolly. The Bible says the "heaven-throned God breaks out laughing" (Proverbs 2:4 MSG). He is never bothered because He always has the right perspective. When we get overwhelmed by life's storms, "God breaks out laughing" at it and us. He's a humorous God.

Interestingly, our English words *humor* and *humility* both share the same root word *hum*. A hum is a continuous low sound like what a humble bee (bumblebee) makes when flying. The humble are low enough to laugh at themselves and the trials of life. Their reference point is God. Knowing the massiveness of God and his grace on them, then knowing the smallness of their problem and its effect on them, they smirk at the problem's implications. Have a cheerful disposition where laughs come early and often. Condition yourself to chuckle. Be willing to look silly to maintain your sanity. The Bible says, "The humble shall increase their joy" (Isaiah 29:19 NKJV). That's why Jesus, the humblest, was anointed with "the oil of gladness more than His companions" (Heb. 1:9 NJK). He was the humblest, so He had the most joy. If you want to increase your joy, have some humble pie.

YOUR BEST FOOT FORWARD

This brings us to a very important point. Like the bumblebee, we need to be humble enough to be our best every day for everyone we encounter. Many opportunities have been squandered and careers ruined because we're not our best. You knew what to say, you knew what to do, but you just didn't say and do it. Whether it was fatigue, hunger, anger, or just a mental slip, not being our optimal selves can cost us more than we want to pay!

As queen, Esther's job was to persuade the king to have mercy and make favorable decisions. She had to be her best every day. She had to be pleasing to the king at all times. Not doing so could have cost her her place in the palace. The previous queen, Vashti, lost her royal position. She refused to come out of her chambers to King Ahasuerus's court for a party he was hosting. Not a good idea. The king was furious. He demoted her instantly, and just like that, her great career was gone because she failed to honor a great relationship (employee-employer). Following her feelings and not being her best cost her her livelihood. The influence she could have had was gone; the people she could have helped would have to be helped by someone else.

I can't help but wonder how many opportunities have vanished before us all because we weren't friendly or because our best foot wasn't put forward. Put your best foot forward in all social interactions. All people are important; God sent His Son to die for them. You know the worth of a thing by how much one is willing to pay for it. We were purchased with the blood of Jesus. Do not squander opportunities—both known and unknown—with important people.

GENUINENESS

I'm not calling Christians to have a getting-over mentality to deal with people only because you think it will benefit you in the future somehow. No, "you can be sure that using people, or religion, or things just for what you can get out of them—the usual variations on idolatry—will get you nowhere and certainly nowhere near the kingdom of Christ" (Ephesians 5:5 MSG). The Lord and people will know when your interest in them is fake, and self-serving. People can smell pride, and if they do, they'll shut down. I'm calling Christians to believe like Christ and develop a genuine interest in people groups of all kinds the way that Mordecai took interest in his little cousin, Esther. I'm call Christians to be class acts, to be known by more people, liked by more people, and respected by more people.

You can't force your way into someone's life, but you can serve your way into it. You just have to study how to serve. The pie will allow your relationships to be organic and not forced. They are to be made intentionally, grown authentically, and maintained genuinely, or discovered, developed, and deepened. There's someone doing what you want to be doing right now. Study them and, if you can, serve them. Learn their methods and take on their habits. Be keenly aware of greatness in your field.

SOME MASTERY

Finally, to have a great career, there is no substitute for time spent in your craft, acquiring excellence. It's what Mordecai did at the king's gate, it's what I was doing as a child preaching in the backyard. Practice purges imperfections and makes things easier. Hang in there. You can get some mastery and acquire genuine connections that will propel you into your great career.

Now let's say you get that, you should be genuine and friendly, learning names, handling people, and studying personality types in your career. But you don't have a job! Now use what you just learned to acquire one.

Once you know what you want to do and you have some level of mastery in that area, prepare yourself to be interviewed. Take interest in the company. Find out a little bit about them, their past and current endeavors. In other words, study to answer them. Own the moment. You'll be confident because of what you know. Information removes doubts and instills confidence. Informed people interview well.

Remember, great people delete discomfort. With genuine friendliness put your interviewer at ease. Let them know these two things:

1. I understand personality types so you can put me anywhere in the company.
2. I will excel at everything I do because I welcome correction.

The former is because you're informed, and the latter is because you're broken. If you say these two things at the right interview, at the right place, at the right time, I guarantee you your great career will ensue.

YOUR PIECE OF THE PIE:
A GREAT VISION

Therefore I was left alone when I saw this great vision,
and no strength remained in me.

—Daniel 10:8 (NKJV)

Wintertime in Martinsville, Virginia, can be fairly frigid. There are some brisk winter nights when the temperature drops below freezing. To counter these cold conditions, my dad used to do what we call "make a fire." In our basement, we had this old black cast iron stove affectionately known to us as the "woodstove." After a couple of planks and logs to start and keep the fire, that woodstove would provide enough heat to make our two-thousand-square-foot home cozy. The one-foot-square vents in the floor of each bedroom upstairs connected the basement to upstairs, allowing the fiery heat to permeate the dwelling.

Our whole house was heated by the high temperatures that woodstove created. In choosing to activate the woodstove, my dad was also choosing the perpetual temperature of the home. The building's wintertime comfort was dependent upon a fire being started and sustained.

In the same way, the warmth of your life's greatness is contingent on you making and keeping the fire of humility going in your heart. I like to say it like this (even though my mom tells me not to): when you choose your life's perpetual humility vial setting, then you've also chosen your life's greatness.

Your humility vial is simply an account of how much humility you currently have. It shows how much humble pie you have eaten. Your perpetual humility vial setting controls how much humility your vial will contain; thus, how humble you'll be. Once you decide that you're committed to perpetually increasing it, then you are simultaneously deciding where the ceiling on your life's greatness is going to be. You're choosing how warm you're going to be. That is, how much glory God is going to get from you, how broad your impact will be, and how much fulfillment you'll experience.

Our woodstove home was built in the mid-1980s. That's before central air-conditioning units were standardized. To change our home's winter air-condition, a fire had to be developed. There was no alternative. Today, there are so many tactics, get-rich-quick schemes, and drugs that promise immediate peace, prosperity, and fulfillment. They won't last long without perseverance, meekness, and brokenness. We need the ever burning yet elusive fire of the pie for total life conditioning. There is no alternative.

All the rooms on the first floor of our home that my parents still live in have electric heating vents alongside the base of the wall, adjacent to the entrance door. Their control panels are mounted on the wall beside the light switch with settings from sixty degrees to eighty-five degrees. The six-inch-by-six-foot floor units barely get their respective rooms warm, and they do nothing for the stairways, upstairs hallway, or basement. They aren't supposed to. They are designed to be quick fixes, an attempt to make single rooms temporarily comfortable.

That's exactly what we get when we pursue the warmth of greatness without the fire of humbleness. We end up with temporary results. Only parts of our lives will be great if our lives are not permeated with humble pie. We'll only get our piece of the pie in part of our lives.

PROCESSED PICTURES

How limited our vision is sometimes. We need to be reminded often of our responsibility to be great, which requires great vision. Not taking responsibility for our vision undermines its importance.

God made us visual beings. We are stimulated by what's visible to us (men more so than women). We process what we see, then we live from that interpretation. To see is to perpetually process pictures. That's how we understand the world around us. To shed light on the last days, God gave Saint John a series of visions. He told him to "write what you see into a book" (Revelation 1:11 MSG). He didn't tell him what to write; he showed him what to write. Pictures are worth thousands of words. Every picture has a message attached to it, and it is our sight that gives understanding. Vision can be the difference between the warmth of greatness and the coldness of mediocrity.

PERCEPTION

Dr. James Merit says that we have an "inflation and a deflation problem. We have an inflated view of ourselves and a deflated view of who God is." He's saying that our perception is all wrong. One of the Hebrew words for vision is *roen*. According to Dr. Strong, its root word means to see, observe, perceive, get acquainted with, gain understanding, examine, look after, see to, choose, and discover. It has to do with perception, current views, vantage points, and what you're aware of. Isaiah uses *roen* in discussing the Israelites seeing, "they err in vision, they stumble in judgment" (Isaiah 28:7 KJV). They had the wrong view of things which altered their reality. The wrong perception guarantees the wrong experiences in life.

Take today in America for example; we are experiencing more freedom, information, technology, travel, entertainment, and medicine than any other time in history. Yet because of the practice of news broadcasts, we bring in gloom while overlooking how blessed we are. We've been privileged for so long that what we enjoy has become common and blurred in the shadow of trouble. We're experiencing stress and anxiety because we have the wrong perspective.

So what is perspective exactly? It's what you detect and observe, what you take notice of. Your perception composes your reality, the way things are to you. It's your vantage point. Actually, it's determining the way you live. It's shown in your interactions with others and God. It's displayed in the choices you make, the people you like, and the ones you dislike.

Do you spend time in prayer every day? Do you attend church faithfully on Sunday mornings and Bible study nights? Do you help anyone besides yourself during the week? If you don't do these things (and you know you should), it's because you don't see them as important enough. You don't discern or perceive their impact. You're living with inferior vision and being a product of our fast-paced world. Usually we don't consistently do what we don't receive immediate gratification from. Since praying, going to church, and helping others don't appear to be components of greatness, we don't assign any priority to them. The way we use our time is indicative of how we view the world.

Our precious perception is bombarded everyday with advertisements for self-improvement and self-pleasure. Our perception is being persistently pressured. We're constantly being advised to fix ourselves without God to see ourselves as mere mortals. We have to consistently choose contentment because every day, we are asked you try another flavor of potato chips, soft drink, candy bar, or dinner entrée. Not to mention buy new cars, jewelries, clothes, workout videos, and equipment. We are being made to be full of ourselves, to overindulge, and ultimately to perceive ourselves disproportionally. No one is promoting delayed gratification for future success. There's no humble pie being served in the marketplace, only the excessive unrestrained fulfillment of our own appetites and whims. Do what you want to do when you want to do it. That is the prideful self-sentiment of our era. It stinks in the nostrils of God. Achievement is fine, but self-aggrandizement is not.

The way our society perceives sin is being softened. Sin is evil with a fatal nature; it's a dishonorable presence in the sight of God. We've chosen not to look at it that way. We only want to feel and do better now by any means necessary without giving an account for our presumptuous actions. We don't want the responsibility that comes with great perception—to foresee what others willingly ignore.

No wonder God's not popular in most circles. He hates sin. Society would have you to think you are not living unless you're sinning. Love yourself! Go in debt to have this life you haven't worked for. That's what we're being told. Our communities, churches, and cities are suffering because of our shortsightedness. It's counterproductive to sustained significance, success, and satisfaction. Remember greatness is birthed from being close to God. You won't be close to Him if you think He's a party pooper.

Your perception of God will determine how close you'll be to Him. Do you see Him as a loving, caring God? If you do, you'll turn to Him for comfort when you need some love. Do you see Him as a wise, willing mentor? If you do, then you'll look to Him when you need some advice. A lot of people see God as angry, unpleasant, uncaring, aloof, and outdated. That's their perception, so in reality, they don't want anything to do with Him, even though His kindness and wisdom is just as available to them. He's just willing and able to help them, but their own perception is preventing it.

This is Satan's delight. He wants us to be concerned with what's happening to us while ignoring God. The problem with that is all our problems and our successes are temporary, while God is external. Our situations are subject to change; God is not. The Bible says of Christians, "We do not look at the troubles we can see now; rather we fix our gaze on things that cannot be seen. For the thing we see now will soon be gone, but the things we cannot see will last forever" (2 Corinthians 4:18 NLT). He already took care of the biggest problem we had—salvation, our external destination. Since God took care of our eternal destination, nothing before eternity is too big for Him! You won't hurt forever, and your troubles won't last. If you can see it, it's subject to change. The Christians' perspective is seeing or being aware of what can't be seen—that is, God and heaven. God's kids' eternal home is heaven because of Christ; that's the awesome Christian reality. The Bible puts it like this, "Don't shuffle along, eyes to the ground, absorbed with the things right in front of you. Look up and be alert to what is going on around Christ—that's where the action is. See things from His perspective" (Colossians 3:2 MSG). Christians are to take on heaven's viewpoint of everything, to have eternity as life's frame of reference. I look at God and then our situation. That's the God perspective—seeing what and how God wants us to see, interpreting life's experiences with the divine reference point.

This doesn't take any guesswork. God has not hidden His views. The Bible reveals God's view on marriage, money, family, government, politics, and eternity. He's not only aware of everything, He knows how everyone and everything should be ran. While praying, the prophet Jeremiah commented, "You are great in counsel and mighty in work for your eyes are open to all the ways of the sons of men" (Jeremiah 32:19 NKJV). God has and always will be acquainted with our ways. "God doesn't miss a thing—He's alert to good and evil alike" (Proverbs 5:3 MSG). There has never been a time in history where God wasn't watching from eternity. He has seen everything that has ever happened in the universe. Frankly, He has never blinked to refresh His eyes. He "never slumbers or sleeps" (Psalm 121:4 MSG). It is the Bible that contains His perceptive wisdom and foresight for man.

That's why it makes sense to take on a biblical perspective. It's rational. Consider this: God's perspective is the only stable view available. Since He is perpetually aware of everything, His vantage point is always appropriate and just. We, on the other hand, see our spouse as a great partner one day, but the next day, we see them as mean and inconsiderate when they offend us. Our present feelings cause us to be shortsighted. We ignore all of our spouse's good quality dealing with them with tainted perception. I'm glad that God is not like that. He's ever aware of our wants, needs, and the greatness that's in us and our spouses.

Satan wants us to live with limited perception, unaware of our great God's presence. Everything that Satan is doing is to get us to live shortsighted like those bound to the system of this world. Yet "practically everything that goes on in the world—wanting your own way, wanting everything for yourself, wanting to appear important— has nothing to do with the Father. It just isolates you from Him" (1 John 2:16 MSG). That's what our perception will conform to if left to the world and Satan. Everything that Satan does is to get you to be shortsighted; everything that the Father does is to get you to be foresighted. All of Satan's efforts are focused on depleting our foresight; all of God's efforts are focused on you gaining foresight.

King Saul had lost his foresight. He got too big in his own eyes. God had instructed him to "attack Amalek and utterly destroy all that they have and do not spare them" (1 Samuel 15:3 NKJV). Well, Saul attacked the Amalekites, but they spared the king, "Agag, and the best of the sheep, the oxen, the fatlings, the lambs, and all that was good, and were unwilling to utterly destroy them" (1 Samuel 15:9 NKJV). Saul, wanting his own way, kept some spoils for himself, and wanting to appear important, he kept the defeated King Agag alive. Who he perceived himself to be stopped him from obeying God. The prophet Samuel said to him, "When you were little in your own eyes were you not head of the tribes of Israel? And did not the Lord anoint you King over Israel? (1 Samuel 15:17 NKJV). He had lost his awareness of God.

See, our awareness of God comes and goes throughout the day because of the steady stimuli from ads and entertainment. They are not all bad, but we don't have to experience them all. We're too fat, our hair's falling out, our teeth aren't white enough, or somebody else has more power, fame, and fortune. We have become so vain. It behooves us to constantly remind ourselves that "there's far more here than what meets the eye. The thing we see now are here today gone tomorrow. But the things we can't see now will last forever" (2 Corinthians 4:18 MSG).

God will last forever. Being anchored in this truth during one of his life's storms, King David objected, "But my eyes are upon You, O God the Lord" (Psalm 141:8 KJV). There was no physical manifestation of God David could look at. He was reminding himself that there's far more to this situation than what meets the eye. He told himself, "If I keep my eyes on God, I won't trip over my own feet" (Psalm 25:15 MSG).

At the end of the day, we can't be overly concerned with what happens in this life. We must fight for perspective. The only reason they get into trouble is because they have given way to shortsightedness. All laws are broken because man has chosen to be aware of his existence without respect to God and other people. He is overly concerned with his life instead of by faith relegating that task to God.

Man is living with distorted views. Without the Christian perspective, man is deceived. He is held captive under a delusion. Without the pie, man is delusional. Strong language, but it's an accurate description of the average American in consumer debt, trying to control other people's perception of them.

DIVINE REVELATION

Another facet of vision is seen in the Hebrew word *maroh*. It denotes a "visionary appearance or prophetic vision and looking glasses" (Strong's Concordance). March is a picture of something that has not happened yet. It's a possibility, but not the current reality. A *maroh* is given to serve as a reality to strive for or a warning to guard against. Either way, when God gives you a vision, it gives context to your life. God has individual looking glasses for all His children to see their world with.

Maroh is used in Daniel 10:8 where he says, "I was left alone when I saw this great vision." Daniel saw what appeared to be a man "dressed in linen, with a belt of the finest gold around his waist. His body was like chrysolite, his face like lightning, his eyes like flaming torches, his arms and legs like the gleam of burnished bronze, and his voice like the sound of a multitude." This usage frightened him. Yet the apparent man explained, "I have come to explain to you what will happen to your people in the future, for the vision concerns a time yet to come" (Dan. 10:14 NIV). He went on to reveal to him all of mankind's history, including Israel's. This great *maroh* was to be the prophet Daniel's life message. He received his looking glasses. The future had been painted.

Daniel's life now had a context. Knowing what was to come of his people, he had a message to proclaim so that Israel and the world might know that God knows "the end from the beginning and from ancient times things that are not yet done" (Isaiah 45:10 NKJV). God made the decision to follow Him easy. Before anything starts on the earth, God is already at the finish line. The evidence that God's going to finish a thing is when He starts it! He completes it, then He begins it. That's why He says, "My thoughts are not your thoughts nor are your ways my ways says the Lord" (Isaiah 55:8 NKJV). He's end of a thing minded. That's context for you.

Prophecy, or knowing the future before it happens, takes supernatural (more than natural) intelligence. Referring to prophecy, Jesus said, "I tell you before it comes, so that when it does come to pass, you might believe that I am He" (John 13:19 NKJV). Jesus's trump card for knowing what to believe in was prophecy. Daniel's vision was prophetic, and it put his life in focus by removing any doubt of the supernatural intelligence of God.

He didn't have to wonder why he was on earth. His vision gave him his importance. Divine importance comes when divine revelation is given. A God vision gives you divine revelation, information that would otherwise be inaccessible. A vision reveals what could happen in the future. It's a possibility, not a guarantee.

Oh, what an awesome God that He would give us a portrait of a possibility to strive for, a picture of an "expected end" (Jeremiah 29:11 KJV) so we can be joyous while we're waiting on the fulfillment of the vision. It's what sustained the Lord Jesus. "He for the joy [of obtaining the prize] that was set before Him endured the cross, despising and ignoring the shame, and is now seated at the right hand of the throne of God" (Hebrews 12:2 AMP). Since Jesus had divine revelation, what He was experiencing (suffering and shame) was in the bigger context of His ultimate triumph. Divine revelation empowers perspective. They work together. Once you know what's ahead, it's easier to look to God while you're waiting on tomorrow.

God gave Daniel a number of visions. He wants to do the same thing for us. God has "looking glasses" for us to behold every area of our lives. This divine perspective causes us to be excited at our job even though we may not like what we're doing, the people we're doing it with, nor the people we're doing it for. It's not going to be forever, so we can bear it. We can be agreeable and cooperate because we have inside information.

King Solomon said it like this, "If people can't see what God is doing, they stumble all over themselves; but when they attend to what

He reveals they are most blessed" (Proverbs 29:18 MSG).

The most blessed people are those who don't stumble over themselves because they see what God reveals. We schedule our own missteps, our own miscues, our own mistakes because we ignore the fact that God is working. God gave Daniel something to look at. He was troubled, but he was attentive and receptive. Jesus had revelation. He was beaten and bruised, but He kept His vision for a greater day out in front of Him. There's revelation for you too. There's room among the most blessed; there's room amongst the great!

FOCUS

Corrected perception and divine revelation allow you to persist and ignite excellence. That's because optimal vision allows you to focus. Anything that doesn't pertain to the vision becomes blurred and out of focus. The vision becomes your life's headquarters by which you run all of your plans by. It's your center to approve or disapprove all your activity. It's where your purpose and plans collide.

We're tempted all the time to lose our focus and "conformed to this world (this age) [fashioned after and adapted to its external superficial customs]" (Romans 12:2 AMP). We do a lot of stuff subconsciously, just going through the motions. Yet if we have a focal point, a picture of where we can go, we are empowered to say no to an extra pair of shoes or a new hat. Those are the material things that should be blurred out of focus. Exceptional people are hit with the same temptations to overspend or drink and smoke and be lazy as common people are. But the great keep their focus. They don't take their looking glasses off.

I have some prescription glasses that I wear sometimes for my nearsightedness. I can see the world in front of me, but anything thirty yards out becomes blurred. I have to strain my eyes to obtain a focus at that distance. My eyeglasses correct my perception, allowing me to have a foresight that's in focus. My problem is I don't like wearing glasses (I don't like anything on my face), so I often put up with my nearsightedness when I know the glasses will cure the problem every time. Without fail, my glasses correct my vision. My struggle is with the small discomfort of having something on my face, so I keep taking them off.

Like my glasses, a vision puts things that are off in the distance in focus so you can see clearly. It will cure your shortsightedness every time. The only trade-off is the restrictions it places on your prodigal living. You won't be able to stay up all night, socializing without conviction because you'll know that that doesn't belong in your future.

Don't be so content with the present that you ignore what God wants you to see. Limited vision equals a blurred, limited life.

For the Ephesians, Saint Paul prayed, "I asked the God of our Master, Jesus Christ, the God of glory—to make you intelligent and discerning in knowing Him personally, your eyes focused and clear, so that you can see exactly what it is He is calling you to do, grasp the immensity of this glorious way of life He has for His followers" (Ephesians 1:17–18 MSG). Paul wanted them to have an immense life in which you would need to know God more and have a cloudless focused vision.

The Apostle Paul didn't want the Ephesians to make decisions based on what's in front of them with their future out of focus. Like the Ephesians, we have to resist making decisions that only consider the next sporting event, movie, or TV program. Without a future focus, we react based on our feelings and what may be urgent, but not necessarily important. Urgent things, our feelings, and moods change day to day, even moment to moment. There's no stable place to focus from within ourselves. We must have a God vision to fasten our attention to.

After seeing the vision God had given him, the prophet Daniel said, "I have no strength left, my face turned deathly pale and I was helpless" (Daniel 10:8 NIV). What he saw and how he felt afterward was so strikingly overwhelming, it was sure to stay with him. His life's focus was assured. He would never forget what he had seen. God wants us with no strength, pale, and helpless after we get a vision, so we will turn to Him for its fulfillment and our rejuvenation. Only the driven, diplomatic, and those able to detach from their own strength will have their dream come to pass.

A GREAT VISION

You know you have a great vision when you can't share it. You find yourself daydreaming about it. A conversation, a book, even an advertisement can trigger our thought of what the future could hold for you. Great mental pictures are powerful; they give you a sense of purpose and destiny no matter how old you are. It's not too late, and it's certainly not too early to be jolted by a great vision.

Not only will a great vision stay with you, but it will involve a lot of people and take God to bring it to pass. God showed Daniel these evil empires that would arise (Persia, Egypt, Syria, and the revised Roman Empire.) Their kings would do great wickedness on the earth: demanding worship, taking money, abusing their power, stealing land, and murdering millions. Allies would have to work together, and God would have to intervene to bring down those tyrants. A great vision requires great human collaboration and the Father (the Great One) to come to fruition. Then as a result, the maximum amount of people are benefited, and the least amount are sorrowed.

A lot of people have visions of getting married, moving their family to a better neighborhood, getting a new house, a raise at work, or a new job. To have these things come to pass is fine. To an extent, they require God, but they only affect you and your family. God wants to display His greatness through us so the world can get exposed to Him. He has more to show us besides a spouse, a home, and a job.

His great vision for you is so massive that it is going to eventually cause you to have energy and tenacity. You will find yourself excited to get out of bed in the morning. It's that type of drive that promotes growth and development in you and others, not just your immediate family.

The Bible says, "No eye has seen, no ear has heard, no mind has conceived what God has prepared for those who love Him but God has revealed it to you by his Spirit" (1 Corinthians 2:9–10 NIV). God wants to show us things that He's not going to show to anyone else (people and places that are assigned to you). Through Holy Spirit, He wants to show us what He has prepared for us (revelation), and He wants us to look at them from His viewpoint (perception) so our interest can be centered (focus). Revelation, perspective, and focus are important more so than creating or getting a new job. Without them, that job will bring you sorrow.

But a great vision will elevate your sorrows. It will also compel others to buy into it. They will want to ignite Holy Spirit in them to see God at work and receive their own revelation and perspective from Him. A great vision gets those connected to it to get their own pair of looking glasses.

It's simple: a great vision will stay with you, affect a great amount of people, and require God to come to pass. We just have to keep seeking God while He aligns the needed victories with the right people for the territory that we are to occupy.

THE PIE'S PLACE

The Father gave a great vision to father Abraham. It was of the stars in the sky—an innumerable amount—representing the innumerable amount of descendants he would have. He showed Jacob some land that He was going to give him and his offspring. Joseph was shown that he would reign over his parents and brothers as he would have authority over most of the world. Ezekiel saw a valley of dry bones come back to life, signaling the resurrection of his family. Daniel and Saint John were given a picture of the "time of the end for some global perspective." Saint Peter were given revelation for his ministry on the equality of all mankind. He concluded that "God shows no partiality" (Acts 10:34 NKJV). He gave all of his servants great visions so they could make optimal decisions. His character, His very nature, won't allow Him to treat us any differently.

The only question is are we humble enough to persevere in meekness and brokenness until, guided by His revelation, we can see from His perspective and have focused activity. Brother Daniel was having his vision explained to him when he was told, "Don't be afraid. From the moment you decided to humble yourself to receive understanding, your prayer was heard, and I set out to come to you" (Daniel 10:12 MSG). Daniel had been praying and fasting for his family (the Jews). They had not been keeping God's commands. Daniel was concerned for them, so he humbled himself with fasting, positioning himself to hear from God. It was after he ate the pie, his great vision appeared.

It's the divine order. When you are low enough to care about other's, God starts to show you things. He wants to reveal to you your place of honor on earth. The Bible has been telling us, "Before destruction, the heart of a man is haughty, and before honor is humility" (Proverbs 18:12 NKJV). Haughtiness brings disastrous scenes, while the pie brings scenes of greatness. As long as we're committed to the pie, we will tap into the countless destiny scenes that God wants to reveal to us.

Remember the pie is a magnet for the voice of God. The Father has spoken in this manner, "Thus, says the High and Lofty One who inhabits eternity whose name is Holy: 'I dwell in the high and holy place, with him who has a contrite and humble spirit, to revive the spirit of the humble'" (Isaiah 57:15 NKJV). God wants to resuscitate, restore, and renew the humble with great visions. Like a magnet, pictures and words from heaven find their way to Humble Drive. The only question is will you stay there long enough to receive them?

POSITIONING

The privilege to see what hasn't happened yet allows the humble to imitate God and begin with the end in mind. With destiny in view, you can refocus on the course you should be taking. My friend, you can refocus if you have had a great vision, and if you haven't, then God is waiting to give you one. Dr. Jesse Duplantis says, "There's no expiration date on a vision. You can get one at nine or at ninety." It's up to you to position yourself on the right road to receive.

Humility is also a clarifier. Without constant amounts of it, you'll live from distorted views. The prideful are, of all men, the most deceived. Take for example Satan; he's still planting thoughts and ideas in people's minds, destroying families, communities, and countries. He thinks he can win against God because he has no humility. He can't see clearly. This is seen in the fact that he was used to accomplish the very thing he wanted to prevent—the salvation of mankind. Had Satan and his followers known, "they would not have crucified the Lord of Glory" (1 Corinthians 2:8 NKJV). They have no clarity because they have no humility. They will never be in position to receive anything from God.

One way to have the clarity that your enemy doesn't have is by talking to God throughout the day expressing your dependence upon Him. While teaching on humility, Evangelist Joyce Meyer said that several times a day, she prays, "Help me, Lord." Hear the pie in that? Though she is living out a great vision traveling the world, preaching the gospel, she's keeping the proper perception. She knows she needs God's continued assistance to walk in righteousness. Sister Joyce would agree that the pie got her the vision, brought it to pass, and is keeping her in it.

Brother Daniel had a habit of connecting with God throughout his day. "Three times a day he got down on his knees and prayed, giving thanks to his God" (Daniel 6:10 NIV). I'm sure he was crying out for God's help in those prayers. His relationship with God landed him in a lion's den and a fiery furnace. Yet his communication with God kept him on Humility Avenue, creating his great perception that sustained him in both the lion's den and the fiery furnace.

In addition to acknowledging God throughout your day, just before you fall asleep, ask God to speak to you during the night. We don't always hear and see as we should while awake. Asking him to speak to you while you sleep communicates your desire for Him and prepares your conscious to receive life revelation. Be willing to write down what you see during the night whether you perceive its origin or connection to your situation or not. Don't miss out on what God has for you. The right revelation will get you to the right things, at the right places, and at the right times.

This chapter highlights the progression of these lessons. When seeking God is our priority, the God kind of life begins to unfold. "So let's keep focused on that goal, those of us who want everything God has for us. If any of you have something else in mind, something less than total commitment, God will clear your blurred vision – you'll see it yet" (Philippians 3:15–16 MSG).

THE DANGER

Nothing but our total commitment to Him will unfold this God kind of life. Jesus said, "If you don't go all the way with me through thick and thin, you don't deserve Me. If your first concern is to look after yourself, you'll find yourself. But if you forget about yourself and look to Me, you'll find both yourself and Me" (Matthew 10:38–39 MSG). I'm tired of finding myself and realizing I've only got me all I can get me. I've got to find God in all my endeavors. Only He has the perception, revelation, and focus I need to fabricate and facilitate the warmth of greatness.

When your life starts warming up, your purpose has been clarified, you have direction, and you're empowered to perform beyond your resources. You are then prepared to walk into your calling driven, diplomatic, and detachable. However, there is a danger to guard against—the temptation to abort the process to get to what you see. When God reveals a vision, we see it in the present, and the immediacy of it makes us want to make the future vision a current reality. Just be patient! Keep making optimal decisions. For the process doesn't always look like the promise!

YOUR PIECE OF THE PIE: A GREAT MIND

This man Daniel, whom the king called Belteshazzar, was found to have a keen mind, and knowledge, and understanding, and also the ability to interpret dreams, explain riddles, and solve difficult problems. Call for Daniel and he will tell you what the writing means.

—Daniel 5:12 (NIV)

Remember that the first aspect of greatness is when God gets the most glory. It's all about the glory! The scripture says to "give unto the Lord the glory due His name" (Psalm 29:2 NKJV). It's a call to think, speak, and act in a manner that honors Him. The problem with pride is you cannot give God any glory while you're in it. Nothing you consider, say, or do while you're in it will glorify God. Pride is the self-seeking device. It absorbs all the glory, leaving God as an afterthought. It's a dangerous device because God said, "I will not give my glory to another" (Isaiah 48:11 NKJV). He alone deserves the glory, and we can only give it to Him from Humble Drive.

Sadly, our world is more depleted of humility today than any other time in history. No other society has been catered to as much as ours. More people feel entitled than ever before. Egos are bigger, and love is smaller because glory is misapplied. That's why we are so self-conscious, self-centered, self-absorbed, and self-righteous. We seek our own comfort more than the God who gave us the ability to enjoy comfort.

FRAGILE MINDS

It's pride! It's not all arrogance, though all arrogance is pride. Shyness is not arrogance, but it is pride. It's self-centered as opposed to God-centered. Self is the reason for arrogance and shyness. The different faces of pride are causing us to forfeit the greatness that God has for us.

Oh, how pride keeps us acting like we've got it all together when our minds are full of turmoil. Many of us are just hoping that those around us don't figure out that, in all actuality, we don't have it all together. Oh, how fragile our minds are. We're always playing out possible scenarios in our heads; the mind is constantly exhausting itself, leaving us often worried. Everybody is unstable to some degree. We are all indecisive, and we've all done things that we just can't justify.

There are more people taking psychotropic drugs today than ever before because we are not dealing adequately with the pressures of life. We don't need pills for everything. I understand when there is a chemical imbalance, and you need medication to help you produce dopamine or serotonin. But just because you have dark thoughts doesn't mean you need an antidepressant. The side effects alone should keep you at bay—confusion, mood disturbances, vomiting, drowsiness, and even suicidal thoughts. Now think of that—a pill meant to help improve your standard of life could possibly cause you to take your life. Now there are pills prescribed to alleviate the side effects of the antidepressant prescription!

God has a prescription for our fragile minds because if we can excel in our minds, we can excel in every area of our lives. I remember hearing Dr. Murdock say, "I will never have more money in my closet than I do in my bookshelf." I thought, *What an audacious statement!* but I quickly recognized the wisdom in his words. A big closet, small library ratio displays a misplaced priority because your mind is more important than your body. Your mind is more important than your job because if you prosper in your mind, your job performance will prosper. Your mind is more important than your family because if you can take care of your mind, you can take care of your family. If you can excel in your mind, you can excel in every area of your life.

To excel in your mind is to conceive and ponder on driven, diplomatic, and detachable things. When you think great, the maximum amount of people will be helped, and the least amount will be sorrowed.

DANIEL THE DIPLOMAT

Daniel had great thoughts. He didn't forget God. During a royal temptation to violate God's dietary laws, "Daniel purposed in his heart that he would not defile himself with the portion of the king's delicacies nor with wine which he drank" (Daniel 1:8 NKJV). The king's delicacies and wine would have most likely been dedicated to false gods. Daniel's heart (the center of his mind) was calibrated to the heart of God. He didn't reverence the king's false gods. He was a diplomat for God. He knew that God hates sin. He didn't want any part in dishonoring Him. In that moment, he was mindful of God's feelings. Great minds stay mindful of the heart of God.

Daniel's refusal was remarkable because not eating what the king put before him could have spelled death for him and his contemporaries. You see, this was the Babylonian King Nebuchadnezzar before he was humbled. Nasty fellow, he was. He had taken over Judah which is where he acquired Daniel as one of his captive councilmen. The king wanted all his staff to be vibrant and intelligent. They had to go through three years of training to learn the language and the literature of the Babylonians. Their diet was prescribed for their strength and vitality to glorify the false gods. How offensive the denial of these delicacies must have been.

But that's what operating at greatness looks like—competent diligence applied to protecting their relationship with God. Taking this kind of stand for God was proof that pleasing Him was important to him, even in the face of humiliation and potential death. After that, Daniel the Diplomat was sought-after to interpret some handwriting on the king's plastered wall. "This man Daniel, whom the king called Belteshazzar, was found to have a keen mind, and knowledge, and understanding, and also the ability to interpret dreams, explain riddles, and solve difficult problems. Call for Daniel and he will tell you what the writing means" (Daniel 5: 12 NIV). He not only loved God, but Daniel was competent as well. He was called for because he was able to solve the problems of Nebuchadnezzar's kingdom. His mind was up for the challenge in part because he wasn't a part of the riotous living in the kingdom. Wrongdoing clogs the mind, stopping you from being your optimal self. The greatest rendition of you will not be expressed unless you resolve to take a stand against sin.

No act of sin is insignificant. King Solomon said, "Catch us the foxes, the little foxes that spoil the vines, for our vines have tender grapes" (Song of Solomon 2:15 NKJV). He calls for the capture of the "little foxes." Not the full-grown ones, not the strongest, most vicious ones but the little ones. They are well capable of destroying the luscious harvest of grapes. In the same way, little acts of sin can destroy our harvest, that is the life that we could have. It is the small errors in judgment that keep us from our optimal lives. Never forget that no act of sin is insignificant.

When our little foxes are caught, we move closer to helping the maximum amount of people and harming the minimum amount. In Daniel's case, he interpreted the writing, so the maximum amount of people were helped (the king and his subjects), and the minimum amount of people were sorrowed (the Hebrew slaves).

It was a mind set to stay away from sin that held the answer to the king's problem. Is your mind set to answer any royal problems? What realms of greatness are you being denied because of your suboptimal decision making?

The Bible says that "the wages of sin is death" (Romans 6:23 NKJV). Sin is the death agent. It kills the life that God wants us to have. Every time we sin, we forfeit part of our destiny. I believe in the grace of God, but the truth remains that we determine how much glory God is going to get out of our lives. Every day we decide how much of our purpose we're going to trade away. Every act of sin robs us of who we could be. I wonder how much of our destiny we have forfeited because of sin paying its wages to us. I'm keenly aware that where I'm going, drugs and alcohol can't go. Lying and lust aren't welcome. My destiny won't accommodate them. My future won't accommodate any thoughts or activities that don't glorify Him.

ADAM AND EVE'S CHOICE

The first part of a man to be attacked was his mind. The instrument was "the tree of knowledge of good and evil" (Genesis 2:9 NKJV), the culprit was Satan, and the victim was the first woman, Eve. God commanded Adam and Eve not to eat of that tree, but Satan refuted God's authority and tricked Eve into eating the forbidden fruit. "Then she gave some to her husband, who was with her and he ate too" (Genesis 3:6 NLT). Instantly, they were aware of themselves and the potential of evil in their perfect world. At that point, they died spiritually, and their minds, wills, emotions, and bodies began to deteriorate. They said yes to Satan, and as a result, it's even harder for us to say no to him because all of our encounters with him are from the fallen state.

The Father would walk in the garden with them enjoying their company. He would have taught them everything they needed to know and anything they wanted to know. Yet temptation allured them away from their relationship with Him because they sought information apart from him. The tree of knowledge of good and evil falsely advertised some secret knowledge God was withholding from them. Being deceived by the salesman, Satan, they conveniently ignored God's central goodness, which is the context for all that is good and evil. They were free to be brilliant, but they willfully bought into sin, binding them and us to thinking and doing wrong.

After four thousand years of this thinking and doing wrong, Jesus, the great high priest, appeared. Not "a high priest who is unable to sympathize with our weaknesses, but one in every respect has been tempted as we are, yet without sin" (Hebrews 4:15 ESV). Jesus never did anything evil. His great mind held up against temptation. Aware of that, the Apostle Paul says to "let this mind be in you which was also in Christ Jesus" (Philippians 2:5 NKJV). Jesus chose God over sin in everything He thought and did. That's when greatness is clearly seen; when you could choose to think and act outside of the will of God, but like Jesus, you decide to pick God regardless of the temptation.

Adam and Eve were capable of doing the same thing. They were living with great minds until they chose to sin. Every day that they chose God's instructions over temptations, they were displaying their greatness. Likewise, every moment that you choose to consider God's desires over temptation, you are glorifying God, expanding your impact potential, and receiving fulfillment.

Our foreparents' colossal mistake teaches us that not only do you lose when your mind loses, but many unseen people, places, and things lose as well. You don't lose in a vacuum. Their wrong caused everyone born after them to have an uphill internal struggle with putting themselves before God. When you don't excel in the world of your mind, it's going to be hard for you and the people connected to you, both known and unknown. You are guaranteed disproportional hurts, heartaches, and pain when due attention is not given to the mind. It will cost you and your world more than you want to pay.

Adam and Eve thought that their little act of taking a snack on God's time was harmless. Well, it wasn't. It released enduring generational anguish all because they let their minds spend too much time at the wrong site. When their mind was in the right place, all was well, but when their mind was redirected, guess how many people benefited? Nobody outside of themselves. The world was sentenced to a life of sorrow. One act of disobedience can stop you from having what you could have and being who you could be. What are you subjecting your mind to? What pain are you sentencing those around you to? What are you putting in motion for the next generation to deal with?

THE RIGHT ROAD

Adam and Eve left Humble Drive. All instructions are fulfilled from there. In humility, you can obey any oracle, submit to any leader, and love anybody. You have to have some humbleness to do what God's Word says. Jesus "humbled himself in obedience to God" (Philippians 2:8 NLT) because all obedience is fulfilled in humbleness. Satan knows this, that's why all temptation is an attempt to get you off Humble Drive, to stop you from eating Humble Pie.

Satan left that road which is why he was cast out of heaven. He was in leadership in heaven, overseeing the praise and worship until pride was found in him. Not happy with his role, he exclaimed, "I will exalt my throne above the stars of God; I will also sit on the mount of the congregation. On the farthest sides of the North; I will ascend above the highest of the clouds, I will be like the Most High" (Isaiah 14:13 NKJV). A clear contrast to Jesus's words to the Father when He wasn't happy with His current role, "Not as I will, but as you will" (Matthew 26:39 NKJV). Jesus stayed in position to fulfill God's will. Satan's position didn't have enough power for him, so he started pushing his own agenda. Though Jesus felt powerless, He still remained in position to fulfill God's will.

Satan said, "I will, I will." Jesus said, "Not as I will, but as You will." Which phrase do you say more often, "I will" or "Not my will, but as You will"? The answer to that will tell you what road you're traveling on.

HIS MIND

No one was negatively affected by Jesus's mind. All those around Him benefited from His astonishing thinking ability. How can we have this great mind that Jesus had? The kind Adam had when he named all of the animals and tended God's garden? The pie manifesting itself in repentance. That is, repent of your specific sins. To repent means to change your mind about a particular thought, word, or behavior. It means to take on God's hatred for it and to never be in bondage to it again. In that moment, you are marked by the spirit of God. As a result, the Bible teaches that spiritually, "You have the mind of Christ" (1 Corinthians 2:16 NKJV). The spirit of Jesus Christ is in you; you are ever hosting greatness. Now "greater is He that is in you than he that is in the world" (1 John 4:4 NKJV).

All of the answers to all things of all times are already on board. Spiritually, you've already got it all. This is the advantage Christians have. The problem is many do not know what they have and many more know it but aren't living like it. You have to constantly remind yourself that you have access to all the information that is in the mind of Christ.

God reveals plans, ideas, and directions from that reservoir inside us. All Christians can draw from this well, but only those who have a close relationship with Him check in with Him on a regular basis. They are in touch with the God in them. When you are aware of Him in you, you're at an advantage. Living with this advantage is a privilege reserved for God's intimates, those who are humble enough to recognize this spiritual reality continuously.

This is when God is glorified, when we think and speak from this fruitful mind inside us. The Bible ask us to "with one mind and one mouth glorify the God and Father of our Lord Jesus Christ" (Romans 5:16 NKJV).

BRAIN FOOD

Having grown up in church, I often heard from the pulpit "and do not be conformed to this world, but be transformed by the renewing of your mind, that you may prove what is that good and acceptable and perfect will of God" (Romans 12:1 NKJV). I remember hearing this verse used to encourage the congregation to change our minds about sin and start thinking like Christ. I got that I shouldn't let the culture, which changes, determine how I think, but that God's Word, which doesn't change, should be the determining factor for my pondering thoughts. I understood that, but I did not know that the next verse tells you exactly how to transform your thoughts. It reads, "To every one of you not to think of himself more highly than he ought to think, but to think soberly" (Romans 12:3 NKJV). The word is saying that having a humble mindset is the way to renew your mind. It is the key to proving what is that good and acceptable and perfect will of God.

God's perfect will for you is predicated on your commitment to lowering your mind, reining it back in when you've patted yourself on the back after accomplishing something or comparing yourself to someone else. This comparing is not wise because all of God's children have value and the potential to be greater than we currently are. They may have the potential to be more significant to more people than you! It's easy to drift into jealousy or envy right out of God's perfect will for you. To have clarity of His will, the Bible prescribes humble pie—a mind set to start from Humble Drive.

Having this "humbleness of mind" allows you to cast "down arguments and every high thing that exalts itself against the knowledge of God, bringing every thought into captivity to the obedience of Christ" (2 Corinthians 10:5 NKJV). You have to stop prideful thoughts in their tracks, arresting any line of reasoning that goes against the Father's desires. Thoughts of intimidation, shyness, insecurity, and haughtiness all put you ahead of God (stagnating your life). Don't ponder them. You don't have to be the most popular, have the best skills, or have the most knowledge to excel. Greatness is revealed when your mind is content. Then you will pursue the skill set and wisdom you need to give God the most glory.

To function like this, the Bible says, "Summing it all up, friends, I'd say you'll do best by filling your minds and meditating on things true, noble, reputable, authentic, compelling, gracious—the best, not the worst; the beautiful, not the ugly; things to praise, not things to curse" (Philippians 4:8 MSG). That's what great minds do. You have to stay keenly aware of what's going on in your head. If it doesn't fall into this list, it's not worth contemplating. It won't cause you to feel your best. Mental real estate is the most expensive real estate in the world. Don't give yours away.

This is why studying the Bible is so important. It is the foundation of all godly wisdom. It is "true, noble, repeatable, authentic, compelling, gracious, the best and not the worst, the beautiful and not the ugly." It's God's words to mankind. Its wisdom is unsurpassable. Let it speak to you. When you read it, write down what you think the author is conveying, what it means to you, and what it means in its context. "God's word is an indispensable weapon" (Ephesians 6:17 MSG). It will redeem your mind. The word is necessary brain food.

Significance, success, and satisfaction are not sustainable without it. The natural mind is filthy. Loaded with immorality, it needs to be soaked in the Word. We must dump our minds into the Word of God. We have to keep bringing our minds back to the Word's standard. It must be our mind's primary tenant. Jesus says that his words are to be "at home in you" (John 15:7 MSG). The Bible should have residency in your heart. What is at home in your heart? What keeps showing up inside of you? We must be broken enough to choose to think the appropriate thoughts.

That's why church is so important. It serves to dispense the Word in fresh and exciting ways so that members may be set on a path of healthy thinking. Solomon says, "Watch your step when you enter God's house. Enter to learn. That's far better than mindlessly offering a sacrifice doing more harm than good" (Ecclesiastes 5:1 MSG). He wants us to develop our minds, and His house is one of the tools to accomplish that. Less harm would be experienced in the world. The reason we hurt people and get hurt is because our minds are not great in that particular area. We are not mindful of something that would cause harm to another. We either don't know that our actions would cause harm to another, or we know but deliberately choose not to be mindful of it. I pray that our church be open brainwashers. We've got to sanitize our dirty mentalities.

This kind of sanitation requires the Word to be taken with the pie. It causes the Word to take root in you. Saint James says to "get rid of all uncleanliness and the rampant outgrowth of wickedness, and in a humble (gentle, modest) spirit receive and welcome the Word" (James 1:21 AMP). The brain needs to be washed thoroughly from its clingy uncleanness; this gentle and modest spirit has to be present for us to receive. The Bible is to be approached with a humble attitude. One that's willing to embrace correction, increase in faith, and acquire more discipline. The Word has the power to clean our minds, but only humility positions us to receive the thoughts that will stay in our mental rotation. There are great songs and biblical lines that have to be mainstays. The pie acts as an adhesive for great thoughts such as:

- "God is great"—to keep you encouraged
- "I'm more than a conqueror"—to keep you focused
- "God is at work"—to keep life in perspective
- "Father, what do I say?" and "Father, what do I do?"— for direction
- "God, I trust you"—(my favorite line) to restore peace We must feed our brains these thoughts daily.

Now if you're too prideful to keep these thoughts on repeat, then you won't recognize God. By default, you will function as your own god with limited information. That's foolish living. Solomon says, "If you think you know it all, you're a fool for sure" (Proverbs 28:26). You will think there is no God, or you'll recognize Him but think that He's not so hot because you don't feel like a conqueror, or you can't get any direction from Him. That's a mind that's sure to produce mountains of frustrations, disappointment, and bewilderment—everything God does not want us to have.

He wants us to be whole, steady, and on our feet. Isaiah said to God, "People with their minds on You, You keep completely, whole, steady, on their feet because they keep at it and don't quit" (Isaiah 26:2 MSG).

To have a great life, your mind has to operate at greatness with God more than it operates at mediocrity. That's the mark of soundness. Solomon says that, "A sound mind makes for a robust body, but runaway emotions corrode the bones" (Proverbs 14:30 MSG). You can stop your bones from corroding by being more conscious of what is playing in the theater of your mind. "Sound thinking makes for a gracious living" (Proverbs 13:15 MSG). It's yours through "humble contemplation" (1 Timothy 2:2 MSG). That's God's prescription, not a handful of pills.

WISDOM FOR THE HUMBLE

Daniel said of King Nebuchadnezzar, "His mind hardened in pride" (Daniel 5:20 KJV). That was the conception of his troubled, foolish ways, his prideful mind. He was an example of what Solomon said, "When pride comes, then comes shame, but with the humble comes wisdom" (Proverbs 11:2 NKJV). If you have shame, it's because you're prideful, period. Nebuchadnezzar was put to shame. He lost everything for seven years because he was prideful. Shame always follows pride. The parallel truth is wisdom always follows humility. Humility is the currency that keeps the reception center of the heart open for the occupant of wisdom.

Stay on Humble Drive long enough, and it will lead you into understood information that you can apply. Before Christ came, Solomon was known as the wisest man on earth because He was humble enough to ask God for that wisdom.

Saint James advises, "If any of you is deficient in wisdom, let him ask of the giving God [who gives] to everyone liberally and ungrudgingly, without reproaching or faultfinding, in it will be given him" (James 1:5 AMP). God is longing to be generous with His sorrow-free wisdom. He knows everything about all situations while we know less than we think we know about our own situations. He knows how everything is going to unfold, but He's only dispensing wisdom liberally to Humble Drive. Get there without hesitation and without doubting. If you don't, you won't receive this help from the Lord. Saint James would call you "a man of two minds (hesitant, dubious, irresolute), [he is] unstable and unreliable and uncertain about everything [he thinks, feels, decides]" (James 1:8 AMP). Pride causes us to be doubleminded.

Be willing to ask and be willing to wait on God's wisdom.

The world is not asking God for His wisdom; that's why you can't trust them. If your counsel is not consulting God, then they are doubleminded themselves. Your doctor wants to prescribe you some medication, but how stable is he or she? Do they know the mind fixer? I'm not against getting advice from a non-Christian, but if you can help it, have all your council come from those who believe in hearing from God. Surround yourself with the humble.

I've learned that the humble get wisdom because there is no plate that they won't eat off of. They have resolved that information is worth acquiring from any source, anywhere, any time. They're always adding value to themselves. You have to be willing to receive from different sources on different terms.

It's the mark of the intelligent. They are skilled gatherers of truth. "An intelligent person is always eager to take in more truth; fools feed on fast food fads and fancies" (Proverbs 15:14 MSG). You don't have to have a high IQ to get some expertise in life. You only have to have an appetite for more wisdom. We must be given to it. "Give yourselves to disciplined instruction; open your ears to tested knowledge" (Proverbs 23:12 MSG). Some people receive instruction for a while, but they don't give themselves to it. We've all started getting instruction or correction in some area, whether it's a diet, budget, prayer, or Bible study plan. We often practice a discipline long enough to be discomforted by it, but not long enough to reap its full rewards. We participate while it's painful, but we don't persevere to the prize. We don't have to keep coming up short. The prize is ours for the taking because the pie is ours for the eating. Wisdom to fulfill the call of God on your life is at your disposal.

College, trade schools, certificate programs, and seminary are awfully important. They make us more useful to the world around us. They won't increase your EQ, which you will need to succeed, but they will expose you to an array of information and ways to process it. I know everybody can't afford to attend a university. Actually, it's said that the average cost for college has gone up 500 percent since 1980. Yet the humble are not deterred. There are more books and free information available today than ever before. The Internet has some answers for competent, diligent seekers.

The wise stop and ponder over any new knowledge. There is wisdom for character and skillful living in your marriage, finances, and career. Press your way to the wisdom that will cause you to excel. Have a prayer life and be rooted in a local church. That's wise. The people in Jesus's hometown inquired, "How did He get so wise" (Matthew 13:54 MSG). He was well read, He had a prayer life, and He was rooted in His local synagogue.

A FIXED MIND

When asked by a lawyer, "'Which is the greatest commandment in the law?' Jesus said to him, 'You shall love the Lord your God with all your heart with all your soul and with all your mind. This is the first and greatest commandment'" (Matthew 22:36–38). This command calls for one to get closer to God. When your mind is fixed on loving God, the mind of God gets fixed on bringing you greatness. Daily you will be tempted to envision things that God hates, but stay in the low place. Stay in love by considering only what He approves of. That's how greatness gets in your life. It starts in the mind.

When our brain is saturated with the pie, we will see how needy we are. We need information, systems, and people. Lord, help us to soar mentally just as Jesus did. "Since Jesus went through everything you're going through and more, learn to think like Him. Think of your sufferings as a weaning from that old sinful habit of always expecting to get your own way. Then you'll be able to live out your days free to pursue what God wants instead of being tyrannized by what you want" (1 Peter 4:1–2 MSG). When we think like Jesus, freedom floods into every area of our lives. You need mental clarity in your home? On your job? At your church? Pursue what God wants instead of being tyrannized by what you want. He wants you to succeed in your home as a great parent and on your job as a great employer or employee and at your church as a servant of His. So categorize your current "sufferings as a weaning from that old sinful habit of always expecting to get your own way." The sooner you wean; the sooner your life can beam with increased greatness.

Throughout the day, train your mind to come back to what God wants done in this moment. Ask God to show you how He can get the most glory in this situation. Remember, it's all about the glory. That's the cure for mental mediocrity, a fixed saturated mine.

CAUTION

Remember, I'm not opposed to receiving psychiatric help. You may need to get some Christian counseling. I'm just calling you to recognize the power of the Word. God's message to mankind is still relevant today. Unlike the United States constitution, the Word doesn't need to be amended or updated. It was true when God had it recorded for us two thousand years ago, and it is true now because God is truth.

I also want the children of God to be aware of their bodies. That mental agitation and anguish can be due to lack of sun exposure, sleep, or the American diet. Our brains won't be optimal with four or five hours of rest, low water intake, plenty of sodas, chips, cookies, pastries, pizzas, and hot dogs. Most of us need a good seven hours of sleep a night and a brief nap during the day to be our best. We all need a diet full of real food to fuel our bodies (fruits, vegetables, nuts, and berries).

I'm a big advocate of eating according to your blood type. Just as there are four different body blood types (O, A, B, AB, with a positive or negative designation), we metabolize food primarily in four different ways. This is due to the thickness variations in the bloods and the sensitivity levels of the digestive tracts. Bro. Joseph Christiano, ND, CNC, would call it eating "genetically not generically." There is no one generic diet that fits everybody. It's eating in alignment with how God designed us individually. Think about it, four people can eat the same healthy skinless chicken dinner and afterward feel four different ways. One is sleepy, one is nauseated, one is energetic, and one is still hungry—seemingly unaffected. The skinless chicken isn't bad for anyone, but it may not be optimal for everyone's particular blood type. Many are discovering that this lifestyle of eating is worth looking into.

Then we all know we need some exercise during the week to strengthen our bodies. The Bible says, "Workouts in the gymnasium are useful" (1 Timothy 4:8 MSG). I like working out in the comfort of my home, but don't curse the gym. Surprising improvement would be realized if we simply adhere to God's desire for our health and nutrition. Work with God's masterful design so your mind can work masterfully for you. There is no room for laziness when it comes to having a great mind. Don't just dig a fork into the pie, dig deep inside your humility vial and persevere. You can do it! Seek first to address all mental problems with the Word, exercise, diet, and nutrition. The world of your mind is awaiting enlargement. A great mind is a part of your piece of the pie.

YOUR PIECE OF THE PIE:
GREAT FAITH

Only speak a word and my servant will be healed... When Jesus
heard it He marveled and said to those who followed 'assuredly I say
to you I have not found such great faith, not even in Israel!

—Matthew 8:8–10 (NKJV)

Faith is the posture of greatness. I pray it for my family members every
day. That by faith their lives would glorify God, make an impact in
their sphere of influence, and have fulfillment. That they would grasp
the importance of humble pie so they can get their piece of the pie.

I pray that for them because I know I need to be more driven,
diplomatic, and detachable. I work on the three Ds every day so I don't
absorb any glory. Jesus said, "He who speaks from Himself seeks his
own glory, but He who seeks the glory of the One who sent Him is
true" (John 17:18 NKJV). I might say that I want God to be glorified or
"to God be the glory" because it's the right thing to say when God has
been honored through me. I want those words to be the true intention
of my heart. But I know that the more I grow, the more the potential
to be deceptively prideful grows. Shamefully I've sought my own glory,
but in my mind, I justified it because I needed to be impressive so I
could expand my influence. That way, the maximum amount of people
can be benefited. While that reasoning is noble, it is inaccurate because it's not my responsibility to identify everyone who's a part of the
maximum amount of people whom I am to benefit. It's God's responsibility. My responsibility is to have faith in God, and He'll expand
my influence. If I make optimal decisions, He'll awaken people to me!

THE TRUST FACTOR

There's a worldwide famine of faith. This was Jesus's concern when He asked, "When the son of man returns how many will He find on the earth who have faith?" (Luke 18:8 NLT). He knew this era would come. We rely on our own strength and intelligence instead of having faith in God, the giver of strength and intelligence. That's because "there is a root of sinful interest in us" (Galatians 5:15 MSG). We are prone to order our own steps. We're accustomed to trusting ourselves.

The Bible declares, "Trust in the Lord with all your heart, and lean not on your own understanding; in all your ways acknowledge Him, and He shall direct your paths" (Proverbs 3:5–6 NKJV). We have the opportunity to have our paths directed by the Great One. His requirement is that we have faith in Him. When others are frantic because they've been laid off, they're experiencing a medical condition, or a nasty divorce, the children of God can still have hope because they have faith in Him. They can believe for the path to a greater job, a greater body, or a greater marriage.

Jesus knew that the last days would produce so much tragedy and trouble that people would lose their faith in God because they can't see Him nor sense Him working. Trust that the Lord will bring you through life's storms. Victory is yours. Resist the very thing that will connect you to your destiny, having faith, the posture of greatness.

"This is the victory that has overcome the world-our faith" (1 John 5:4 NKJV). Faith is the victory over your problems. So when you're tempted to let go of your faith because you're losing in life, that temptation is actually an enticement to let go of your victory. Faith is not believing hard enough until something happens. Faith is believing from the place that it has already happened, that you've already won. Faith is acknowledging the undefeated God in all your ways. It is trusting the flawless victor. Don't let go of your victory!

You initiate victory when you "trust in the Lord with all your heart" (Proverbs 3:5 NKJV). The Hebrew word for trust is *batach*. It's an action word that means to take refuge quickly, to be confident or sure, to be reliant and unsuspecting. Jesus wants people on earth to turn their attention to the word quickly with confidence and assurance. When life happens, consider first what matters to God. He is the ultimate safe haven. "He is a shield to those who trust, and take refuge in Him" (Proverbs 30:5 AMP). The safest thing you can do in life is confidently, unsuspectingly turn to God.

God is trustworthy, unfailingly dependable. You never have to be suspicious about His reliability. "God's reputation is twenty-four-carat gold, with a lifetime guarantee" (Psalm 19:9 MSG). It's already been proven. Our existence is proof of His commitment to us. This is why it's an honor and a delight to have faith in God. He's been receiving trust longer than anybody! He's empowered to work on in your life through your faith in Him. Your faith doesn't give Him any power, but it gives God access to your life. He wants us to trust Him because He wants to help.

Wanting us to get that help, Jesus tells us to "have faith in God [constantly]" (Mark 11:22 AMP). We are to put and keep our stock in God to receive His protection, provision, and power. He's waiting on our trust.

When I think I've got everything figured out, then I have an inferior life because I feel my trust in Him is not necessary. My life is no greater than my time, my abilities, and my resources. It's no bigger than my hands can make it. It's a life that doesn't glorify God. It's a lesser life than what we're meant for. The problem is so many people, both Christians and non-Christians, have been operating without faith for so long that it's normal to trust themselves above all else. They don't know the enjoyment they're missing out on, so they are hesitant to take on God's way of doing things. That would require giving up the comfortability of the known. I don't want an inferior life. I want to have and be everything God has and wants me to be. There in His satisfaction.

GOD'S DELIGHT

Remember that satisfaction is your self-value; it's your delight, your contentment. Success is your value to others; it's others' delight, your conduct. Significance is your value to God; it's His delight in you, your character. We are such disappointments. What could we possibly do to cause God to delight in us? What makes Him smile?

The author of Hebrews tells us, "But without faith it is impossible to please and be satisfactory to Him. For whoever would come near to God must [necessarily] believe that God exists and He is the rewarder of those who earnestly and diligently seek Him [out]" (Hebrews 11:6 AMP). He only smiles when faith is in every scene of our lives. He derives pleasure from His children living with an awareness of Him even though He's the "invisible God" (Colossians 1:15 KJV). That's faith—doing everything knowing that He's watching, trusting the unseen Creator. It's the connection He wants with you. When you don't obey His command to "in all your ways acknowledge Him" (Proverbs 3:6), it hurts Him. He feels pain from our lack of trust during the day. The only way to have Him content with us is to rely on Him. Think of that. He is only happy when we're doing the best thing we can do for ourselves—trusting in Him.

It's the desire of every great parent for their child to conduct themselves in such a way that honors them. That they would act the same way in and out of their presence. They live confidently knowing that their necessities are covered because they have made their parents their refuge. It would be an absolute insult to the parent if the child didn't trust them to take care of all their necessities because the parents know that they're responsible for and more than able to provide the protection and provision the child needs.

In the same way, God is displeased when we live as if He's not a great Father, never consulting Him like He's not around or interested in our welfare. His inexhaustible resources and His ability to get them to us makes our needs pale in comparison. He wants us to live confidently knowing that He's got us covered. Our faith in Him honors

Him because it acknowledges His ability and our dependability. The Father wants to be wanted.

Our faith in God communicates how much He's wanted by us. It's the greatest compliment we can give Him. When we don't trust God, it's because we really don't want anything to do with Him. It's the greatest dishonor we can show Him. But to know Him is to trust Him because He is so desirable. That's why the psalmist advised, "Oh taste and see that the Lord is good; blessed is the man who trusts in Him" (Psalm 34:8 NKJV). To taste is to properly try out. A proper sample of God unleashes a flood of His goodness your way. The psalmist was saying just check Him out; His way of living is greater than any other way. It's the way of faith.

Check him out! God has made faith in Him the purchasing agent of His kingdom. It is God's currency. Faith in Him destroys the gap between Him and us, not faith in your abilities, a job, a family member, or a mentor. Not even having faith in your faith will get you anything in God's system, for He is the only one deserving of relentless trust. Having faith in your faith is just another form of trusting in yourself; that's pride. The Christian life is accessed by faith in the Creator. Dr. Murdock says that "the greatest gift that you can give to anybody is the gift of access." God has given us access to Him through faith. That's why the Bible tells us to "walk by faith, and not by sight" (2 Corinthians 5:7 NKJV). Faith is not inferior to sight, even though we're sense oriented. Faith is superior because it gives us the right of passage to God and His plans.

SAVING FAITH

The way of faith just makes more sense than any other way. It's rational. You see, faith is the only virtue that requires you to get outside of yourself and depend on someone else. If being right with God was by any other means, then He would owe us His pleasure, and we would have a reason to pridefully boast. For example, if we could be right with God by our giving, then our generosity would earn our righteousness. Or if it was loving, our compassion would justify us. The same is true for honesty, honor, boldness, kindness, goodness, and even obedience to a set of commandments. Any one of these acts would give us an unfair advantage with God, but "there is no unrighteousness in Him" (Psalm 92:15 NKJV). He's not doing anything wrong. He has made Himself accessible to all by faith. Whosoever will can believe in Him, not just the wealthy and well mannered.

Getting and staying right with God is all His enjoyable work. Saint Paul says of God, "Saving is all His idea, in all His work. All we do is trust Him enough to let Him do it. It's God's gift from start to finish! We don't play the major role, if we did we'd probably go around bragging that we'd done the whole thing" (Ephesians 2:8–9 MSG)! There's no room for bragging with God. Faith makes sure of it.

HE YEARNS FOR FAITH

Our faith is His daily delight. He created us to enjoy our very existence. When the Bible tells us to "walk worthy of the Lord, fully pleasing him, being fruitful in every good work" (Colossians 1:10 NKJV), it is a call to deepen our faith, a call to develop and grow our trust in Him. Our life, our itinerary, our checkbook, and our friends all display our faith level. Where you go, what you spend money on, and who you hang out with is a picture of how much pleasure the Father is deriving from you. He doesn't love believers any more than anyone else; He just enjoys us more than anyone else.

What a thought! To know that the infinite God created us finite beings with the hope that we would discover His desire for our trust. He foreknew before He made us that many of us would reject Him. Yet He created us anyway because His yearning for our faith outweighs the pain He gets from our rejection of Him.

It's why He asks us to forgive others, to obey Him, and to pray.

It requires faith in Him to do these things. To walk in the fruit of the spirit (Jesus's character) and to operate in the gifts of the spirit (Jesus's conduct) both require faith.

FRUITFUL WORKS

Biblical faith being historically scarce makes great faith even rare in the earth. Great faith is above average; it's extraordinary faith. Great faith continues to trust and believe despite evidence to the contrary. It persists even though it might be counterintuitive to do so. "Little faith" (Matthew 8:26 KJV) will run out; it gets exposed when there's no perseverance to fit the bill. Yet great faith is of considerable duration. When it's developed, it remains on the scene.

This lasting faith has the appropriate corresponding actions. It endures because great faith always gets in line with what it believes. The actions serve to reinforce the belief in God. Father Abraham had great faith. He placed his own son on an altar to be sacrificed. That's what made him right with God, his faith's accompanying corresponding action. He believed God would raise his heir back to life if he went through with the sacrifice. His obedience was evidence of his belief. Making this same point, Saint James asks, "Isn't it obvious that faith and works are yoked partners, that faith expresses itself in works?" (James 2:22 MSG).

He continues, "The for meaning of 'believe' in the scripture sentence, 'Abraham believed God and was set right with God,' includes his action. It's that mesh of believing and acting that got Abraham named 'God's friend.' Is it not evident that a person is made right with God not by a barren faith but by faith fruitful in works?" (James 2:23–24 MSG). The only evidence of a fruitful faith is a fruitful work; that's lasting faith.

Let's say you have an estranged father who's a billionaire, and he tells you that he is going to have a couple hundred million dollars deposited into your empty bank account before the week is out. Instantly, your life would change. Your current actions would change to fit your belief in your father, trusting him to fulfill his promise to you. You'd start planning the vacation you have always wanted or looking at a new car and home. You would start considering who you would and would not help. Your works would be different. You would act like a millionaire. You would do anything your now beloved father asked of you, if you believed him. Relentless deeds would follow his proclamation.

Abraham had a relentless deed that accompanied his continued confidence in God. God may have spoken to other men during Abraham's era, but only Abraham had enough faith to do what His rich heavily Father asked of him—sacrifice his son. He was willing to obey God even though his instruction to him was illogical and counterproductive to his promise to be the father of many nations, but he trusted God.

He was persuaded. He didn't have little faith. He took his son up Moriah Mountain and put him on an altar like an animal to be slain. His great faith caused him to submit to God. Then God's provision was revealed, a sacrificial ram was caught in a bush. Unlike other deities in that era, God didn't want Abraham to kill his son. He was going to give His to the world. He wanted the world to know that Abraham was willing. This is why Abraham will forever be known as "God's friend" (James 2:23 MSG). His great faith in God enabled him to have a great life, as evidenced by the glory God got out of his obedience, his impact on the world, and his personal fulfillment.

FAITH OF THE GREAT

Great things have happened throughout history because of great faith. Noah built an ark not knowing if it would rain or if the animals would comply. Moses led the children of Israel through the Red Sea not knowing if the sea would swallow them up or not. King David slayed the giant Goliath not knowing for sure if his arsenal of five rocks would be sufficient. Saint Paul wrote thirteen of the twenty-seven New Testament books. He couldn't have possibly known how many people would adhere to his teaching. Rev. Martin Luther posted his thesis on the Catholic Church's doors, not knowing if he would be martyred for such boldness. They all had remarkable works in spite of the unknown because they had remarkable faith.

GREAT FAITH MAKING WAVES

It's not just miracle workers, giant slayers, and preachers who have summoned great faith. Many lesser known people operated in it. The Bible relays the narrative of a common woman whose daughter was at home severely suffering under demonic attack. She was a Canaanite mother, not an Israelite like Jesus and His followers. This meant that she had no right to a miracle because Jesus was not assigned to her people group. His ministry was limited to Israel because His ministry had to have a focus. You are not called to all groups of people, but you are called to a group of people. Someone will be receptive to your personality and abilities. Jesus would have spent a lot of time traveling if he didn't have a group of people to focus on. This was His first and only trip into Gentile (non-Israelite) territory.

It was the region of Tyre and Sidon. Jesus had "entered a secluded house and wanted no one to know it, but He could not be hidden" (Mark 7:24 KJV). This woman had heard about Jesus going about "destroying the works of the devil" (1 John 3:8 NKJV). No Gentile had provided her with any lasting help, so her new plan was to get this famous Israelite to have mercy on her daughter. News about the Lord's power over demons had surfaced, and He could no longer be hidden. She was fully persuaded that the enduring help that would set and keep her daughter free was present in Jesus.

A fire is self-announcing! When you help enough people, word about you will get out! Jesus didn't have to do any self-promotion. He was a liberating fire! Upon finding Him, she "cried out to Him, saying, 'Have mercy on me, O Lord, Son of David! My daughter is severely demon possessed" (Matthew 15:22 NKJV). Possessors of great faith relentlessly seek out help. There was no social media to disclose Christ's whereabouts, but upon His arrival to that region, He was sought-after and found by fruitful faith.

Even though He heard her desperate plea, "Jesus gave her no reply, not even a word. Then His disciples urged Him to send her away. 'Tell her to go away,' they said. 'She is bothering us with all her begging'" (Matthew 15:23 NLT). It appeared that Jesus didn't want to be disturbed, and the disciples seemed to be annoyed by her request. This perception of Jesus appeared to be confirmed when He looked at her and said, "I was sent only to help God's lost sheep—the people of Israel" (Matthew 15:24 NLT). Why did He say that? He was identifying the scope of His ministry, which didn't include her. It didn't look like this lady was going to receive any help from this Jewish man since He was pointing out their racial difference. I'm sure she wasn't expecting that. She probably wanted Him to come out to her home, but He seemed to be cold and uncaring without words of compassion or love. I would have been deterred. I would have questioned everything I had heard about Him up to that point, but not her.

She persevered through the awkwardness; her faith wouldn't let her be deterred. She got closer "and worship Him, pleading again, 'Lord help me!'" (Matthew 15:25 NLT). She had taken her daughter's victory on as her own. Though she may not have understood His blatant apprehension toward her situation, she did understand her family's need of Him. This was the unknown, but faith was her victory, so she loved on Him with her worship.

She honored Him with her worship, but Jesus seemed to reject it. He doubled down, "It isn't right to take food from the children and throw it to the dogs" (Matthew 15:26 NLT). Her persistence got her in the Savior's presence. Shockingly, He's off-putting just because she's not a Jew. He called her a dog during a time when Jews were thought of as racist. It's almost hard to agree with or understand Jesus's methods unless you are aware that He's the masterful teacher. As such, He was drawing from her a great confession of faith which was needed to cure her daughter.

She was aware of His greatness. I'm sure she could sense His desire to help. His face was glaring with wisdom and compassion. He was clearly communicating His love for her. In response, "she replied, 'That's true, Lord, but even dogs are allowed to eat the scraps that fall beneath the master's table'" (Matthew 15:27 NLT). She didn't take His response as a personal attack like we so often do. I wonder how many victory parades we've missed because we thought we were done wrong? This Gentile woman was all in. She acknowledged His analogy and inserted her point. Children never eat all of their food; their pets are happy to receive their scraps. She knew that scraps from the healing bread would set her daughter free. No Gentile's bread had helped her daughter, so she was dead to the alternative, her daughter's destruction.

His masterful plan for the woman and her daughter came to fruition. "Jesus answered, 'Woman you have great faith! Your request is granted.' And her daughter was healed from that very hour" (Matthew 15:28 NIV). He was willing to heal her the whole time. I can see the disciples' faces; their confusion and misunderstanding had given way to amazement. They didn't have to see the little Gentile girl to know she was healed that very hour. Jesus had answered the prayers of a Gentile. This was something they had only seen one time before for a Roman centurion. What a lesson they learned on that day about great faith. It doesn't matter who you are, your race, your economic standing, your age, or popularity. Great faith overcomes all other factors that would keep you from being effective at the right things, at the right places, and at the right time. It fills in the gap to purchase your breakthrough. We just have to lean into God to grow our faith so we can fulfill the call of God on our lives.

FAITH AND AUTHORITY

A Roman centurion leaned into God. At Capernaum, he came

to Jesus telling Him of his servant who was at home, paralyzed and ready to die. The Lord sensed this Gentile's faith and said to him, "I will come and heal him" (Matthew 8:7 KNJV). He told the Lord of his problem—the medical field had failed his employer—and Jesus agrees to restore his worker's health by coming by and praying for him. In that moment though, the centurion's faith was above average. He knew it would be more efficient for Jesus just to speak the words of healing and his servant would be healed. He knew Jesus didn't have to be there with the servant. He explained, "I also am a man under authority, having soldiers under me. And I say to this one, 'Go' and he goes; and to another, 'Come' and he comes; and to my servant, 'Do this and he does it'" (Matthew 8:9 NKJV). He understood how words from the right person create realities that didn't exist before those words were released. He knew that Jesus was the right person for his problem. His time spent understanding authority was actually time spent understanding the Lord; if He says it, you can guarantee it will be done. When Jesus heard it, He marveled and said to those who followed, "Assuredly, I say to you, I have not found such great faith, not even in Israel!" (Matthew 8:10 NKJV).

Jesus only identified great faith in two people while He was here. It was the Gentile woman and the Gentile centurion. Having heard about Jesus's healing campaign, they meditated on Him and His ability. That grew their faith in Him. It's also interesting to note that because they were non-Jews, they had not been raised under the Mosaic law. They didn't have years of pride built in them because their people had been given the law or because they kept some commandments better than someone else. When Jesus came along, they were broken enough to seek Him out. They knew they weren't deserving of His time. They didn't feel entitled; they were on Humble Drive.

This common mom and commanding man's faith was anything but common. They were driven to Jesus, diplomatic in their approach, and detached from the naysayers. Greatness was displayed through them. Just ask her daughter and his servant. They weren't there to hear their cases pleaded, but they did receive their breakthrough instantly because of extraordinary faith. Persistence still ignites greatness.

You may not be sick or have a demon, but you are probably facing a sick situation or a demonic dilemma. Whether its financial, relational, or judicial, Jesus can handle it. Great faith in Him works from the common mom to the commanding man. They are proof that greatness knows no class. Its shadow can be seen in all walks of life.

THE PIE PROCEEDS GREAT FAITH

One day, Jesus was teaching His disciples about forgiveness, how they should forgive an offense every time with no exceptions. This prompted the disciples to cry, "Lord show us how to increase our faith" (Luke 17:5 NLT). They knew that it would take more faith than they currently had in order to satisfy that standard. If they were going to please God, they were going to need greater faith. They finally realized its importance.

He proceeded to tell them what a little faith could do, "If you had faith even as small as a mustard seed, you could say to this mulberry tree, 'May you be uprooted and thrown into the sea,' and it would obey you" (Luke 17:6 NLT)! When mustard seeds are full grown, they become large trees, serving as habitation for birds of the air and beasts of the field. Mustard seed faith is faith that's pregnant with potential. Jesus reveals the underestimated power of faith that has the potential to grow. If you are a disciple and you speak to what God wants you to speak to with faith, things happen. He affirms the importance of faith before He gives them the formula for adding to it.

The right question had been asked. Now as the Masterful Rabbi that He is, Jesus asked them some questions for their consideration. "When a servant comes in from plowing or taking care of sheep, does his master say, 'Come in and eat with me?' No, he says, 'Prepare my meal, put on your apron, and serve me while I eat. Then you can eat later'" (Luke 17:7–8 NLT). At first glance, this explanation seems out of place. What does the job duties of a servant have to do with increasing faith? Let's keep listening. "And does the master thank the servant for doing way he was told to do? Of course not. In the same way, when you obey me you should say, 'We are unworthy servants who have simply done our duty" (Luke 17:9–10 NLT). He was saying that the same way a servant humbly completes his chores without applause, you have to have the same servant attitude to increase your faith.

You see, the servant came in from his outside work, not to have an iced tea and a La-Z-Boy recliner but to complete his assignments. He had to preserve through the fences of pride, fatigue, and maybe even an injury to prepare his master's meal. The servant's will was broken so he could accommodate his master's will. He was expected to finish his work without praise or approval. He completed his assignments in trust knowing his master had and would continue to provide all his needs after he was served according to his riches. The servant was willingly humble in obedience. To grow your faith, you have to be willingly humble.

I heard John Bevere say that "pride and faith are opposites." It's true. Humility and faith are inextricably connected. The prophet Habakkuk says, "Behold the proud, his soul is not upright in him; but the just shall live by faith" (Habakkuk 2:4 NKJV). He's saying you have the proud over here and those living by faith over there. They never become the same people without faith because the proud won't get off themselves and trust God. Pride and unbelief go hand in hand, so do humility and faith. The proud believe in themselves (their own ability), and the humble believe in God (His ability). Pride and faith are opposites!

You can see this attitude in the Gentile mother. When she heard that Jesus was nearby, she persevered through the fences of racial and gender tension to get to Him. After she got to Him, she had to persevere through the disciples' rejection and the Master's schedule. It was humility and faith. In meekness, she didn't think too highly of herself; she got down and worshiped Jesus. She was also broken. Her daughter was suffering, so for her daughter's health—not her own—she willingly submitted herself to the Lord Jesus, all the while refusing to be offended, insulted, or outraged.

Her prevailing attitude was a humble one. No wonder she had great faith. I know pride will often surface. Those worse parts of us will be exposed; bad days will come. However, our prevailing attitude should be a humble one. The woman's persistence ignited greatness, great faith for her and a great deliverance for her daughter.

Like that mother and centurion, when we let go of our wicked pride, then our hearts will be positioned to receive God's word. The word works best in those who have a humble spirit. This is important because "faith comes by hearing and hearing by the word of God" (Romans 10:17 NKJV). Faith grows when you hear the Word of God, but you must hear with humble ears. You have to sow God's word in the soil of your heart. Then a harvest of great faith will be available when you need it.

This explains why people can hear God's words at church, from family members, friends, TV, Internet, radio, or even from themselves, but their faith doesn't grow. The Hebrew author said of the Jews, "For indeed the gospel was preached to us as well as to them; but the word which they heard did not profit them, not being mixed with faith in those who heard it" (Hebrews 4:2 NKJV). They didn't humbly receive it. Oh, the places in life that pride has stopped us from going. If we could only get out of our own way. That is, get out of unbelief and mix faith with God's truths.

We are bombarded every day with words that deplete our faith. The news, our coworkers, and associates often produce reasons not to believe God. The economy is bad; sickness, natural disasters, violence, and terror are all up. The reports may make sense, but they don't make faith. We must shower ourselves with God's perspective to counter the effects of the evils of our day.

We must train ourselves to immediately revert back to God's words when we hear words of doubt and unbelief. The first thought you can't control, but the second and subsequent ones you can choose. Don't let your doctor, lawyer, or boss have the final say. Ponder no other thought until you consider what God says about the matter. He'll still "never leave you nor forsake you" (Hebrews 13:5 NKJV). He will still "supply all your needs according to His riches in glory" (Philippians 4:19 NKJV), and He's still the God "who forgives all your iniquities" and the One "who heals all your diseases" (Psalm 103:3 NKJV). These promises must live in the forefront of your minds. We must have a way to get God's truth in our head. The word should be strategically placed on our walls, on the refrigerator, information boards, and mirrors. Don't worry about being extreme. This life cause for extreme faith! You need faith every day; "the just shall live by faith" (Habakkuk 2:4 NKJV). To be truly alive with real sanity (significant, successful, and satisfied), trust God above all other voices. That requires humility. It is inextricably connected to the development of your faith. You can't be who God wants you to be with underdeveloped faith. You can't fulfill the call of God on your life with undeveloped faith. Yet we can all have greater faith because we can all find more time for Him. It will be worth it; God will be pleased, and like the Gentile's daughter and the centurion's servant, somebody's situation is going to improve. Somebody is waiting on you to develop your faith.

FAITH AND LOVE

Are you broken enough to trust Him more? Trust comes from the broken place. When you're aware that you're frail and in need of assistance, you trust Him increasingly like a child in a crowded mall. This trust is directly proportionate to my love for God. The Bible speaks of this relationship, saying, "Faith which worketh through love" (Galatians 5:6 KJV). Love makes faith work. To have great faith, you need great love. You may be thinking, "I thought you've been saying that faith works by humility?" It does! Humility is just a branch that hangs on the tree of love. The Apostle Paul gave fourteen characteristics of love to the church in Corinth; among them was this description, "It is not proud" (1 Corinthians 13:4 NIV). Humbleness is a manifestation of love, an extension of it. When you're being humble in the earth, then you're loving Father God in heaven. That love for Him will develop your faith. It will keep your faith working, working on being great.

A GIFT FROM THE HOLY SPIRIT

One Friday morning, some fifteen years ago, a group of about twenty-five guys, including myself, was gathered for a "Prayer and Share" session at Nottoway Correctional Center. It was an informal setting to discuss any current troubles or triumphs. This particular morning, Bro. Fred Tatrallee was unusually quiet. We were about to close when I touched his shoulder compassionately and asked, "What's going on, Fred? Put me in your world." He told me he was having stomach trouble; he couldn't keep any food down. In fact, he hadn't had any solid food in over three months. He didn't know what was wrong; he was just waiting to see a doctor that Monday morning. I sensed faith arising in me. I asked him to share it with the group. He did. Then I asked the brothers to lay hands on Brother Fred as I began to command his pain to cease and his stomach to function properly.

After my prayer, I told him to take it by faith. We departed, and I didn't see Brother Fred until the following Friday morning. He then announced that the Lord had healed him! He cancelled his doctor's appointment and had himself some steak. It was a miraculous turn-around!

I'll never forget that miracle because I was just a twenty-year-old kid. I was spending time with the Lord daily, but I didn't know that I had developed my faith enough to see a life-threatening ailment healed. Yet in that moment, it was a gift from Holy Spirit, a supernatural importation of faith, allowing me to believe God to do what he wanted to do anyway, heal Brother Fred. In listing the gifts of the spirit, Saint Paul said that the "Spirit gives great faith" (1 Corinthians 12:9 NLT). If a situation arises and no one has grown enough faith to fit the bill, He won't be restrained by our limitations, so as a gift, He'll let us believe Him to accomplish His will. He supernaturally increases our capacity to trust Him so He can get the glory. There is always grace available for our insufficiencies. Oh, what a gracious God. I pray that we would be humble enough to let God solve all the problems through us that He wants.

Now when this gift of great faith that you haven't labored for shows up, it will always be accomplished by a gift of healing, a miracle, a prophecy, or a tongue and an interpretation. Great faith comes to usher in a manifestation of God on earth. It doesn't come by itself. When great faith shows up, the great God shows up!

The pie will make us the believers that we ought to be, but until we get there, great faith is available to the body of Christ. Like that Friday morning, we just have to act the way the Lord would if He was here. Cast out devils, heal the sick, and raise dead people and dead situations. That's what great faith is for, acting on behalf of Jesus in the earth to display all of heaven's greatness until Jesus returns. That's part of your piece of the pie!

YOUR PIECE OF THE PIE:
GREAT POWER

And with great power the apostles gave witness to the resurrection of the Lord Jesus. And great grace was upon them all.

—Acts 4: 33 (NKJV)

America's thirteen colonies formally declared their independence from Great Britain on July 4, 1776, through the Declaration of Independence. Now every fourth of July, Americans celebrate usually with an assortment of fireworks. America expanded her land (from sea to shining sea), her technology (electrical grids), her manufacturing (assembly lines), and her military (intelligence). She is a superpower! She has the ability to make things happen in the world because of her money, counsel, and military presence. She doesn't always make the right moral, economical, or foreign policy decisions, but by the grace of God, she is still a superpower.

She knows her status, so she doesn't ask for permission or help to optimize what's hers. She has as a nation what most people want individually—the ability to make themselves and their environment better. We're longing for better options for our relationships, finances, careers, and health. We want to be empowered.

We have talked for long enough. Now "God's way is not a matter of mere talk; it's an empowered life" (1 Corinthians. 4:20 MSG). He wants our lives to be defined by power. The same way that America is a superpower in the natural, God wants us to be a superpower in the spiritual realm so we can impact our natural world.

Millions of self-help and how-to books have been sold because people want power. We want power to control the unfruitful and dead parts of our lives. There is temporary motivation from these books. They have suggestions and strategies but no lasting inspiration to continue implementing them. There's no power to stay the course. The beauty of humble pie is it provides the strength to do what you know you should but lack the fortitude to do. Brokenness opens you up to receive divine enablement for your daily, weekly, and annual assignments.

FIRM FORCE

Asa was Judah's third king. His army was 580,000 trained men. Wanting Judah's land, Zerah (king of Ethiopia) attacked them with an army of one million men and three hundred chariots. Chariots were the advanced weaponry of the day. To have three hundred of them meant you could advance on your enemy with up to six hundred men already in fighting position with the speed of a horse. They had a super army that almost doubled Judah's. Judah needed the Lord again. After King Asa deployed his armies for battle, he "cried out to the Lord God, 'O Lord, no one but you can help the powerless against the mighty! Help us, O Lord our God, for we trust in you alone. It is in your name that we have come against this vast horde" (2 Chronicles 14:11 NLT). King Asa analyzed his troops and King Zerah's troops. He concluded that Zerah's was mighty and his was not, so he called on the almighty God.

Kowach is the Hebrew word for power used here as the root of powerless. Kowach means to be firm, vigor, force. Figuratively it means capacity, means, and produce (Strong's Concordance). Unlike America, the Judean troops didn't have enough firmness, strength, might, nor did they have the capacity or means to produce or carry such force to their mighty opposition. I know a lot of people are living life like this—powerless. They have no mental, physical, or spiritual power to combat the might of fear, poverty, sickness, and disease. Judah didn't have kowach; they were soft and vulnerable. They didn't have enough vigor and lacked the hard numbers and technology to apply firm force to their opponent. Yet what they lacked in power, almighty God would make up the difference.

Kowach emphasizes the solid nature of power. It makes you confident and steadfast in the face of trouble because you're aware of the ability that's available. King Asa knew they didn't have that ability, so he put his faith in the Father, declaring, "It is in Your name that we have come against this vast horde" (2 Chronicles 14:11 NLT). He allowed God to be responsible for the battle by hosting it in His name. He was calling in firmness that they didn't have so they wouldn't have to be nervous and afraid.

AUTHORITY

In closing his second letter to the church at Corinth, Saint Paul enlightens them, "I write these things being absent, lest being present I should use sharpness, according to the power which the Lord hath given me to edification, and not destruction" (2 Corinthians 13:10 KJV). The apostle was conveying his erroneous tendency to be brash because he was authorized by the Lord to speak truth and correct error in their lives. He only wanted to encourage them (replenish their courage). For the word *power*, Saint Paul uses the Greek word *exousia*, which—according to Dr. Strong—denotes "authority, leave or permission, liberty of doing as one pleases." This power that Saint Paul had wasn't his ability to speak, demonstrate, or stand firm, but it was his right to do so.

Exousia comes from the verb *exesti*, which means "it is lawful." Those with exousia have legal permission to act as they please on behalf of the one who authorized them. They have the law behind them, backing their every decision. Great responsibility comes with having this kind of power. Only those who can be trusted to carry out the will of the one who gives this power will have it. After a police officer has been trained, he is then trusted by the city, county, state, or the federal government that trained him. They give him a badge with which he can act on behalf of that jurisdiction. When it's in the law's best interest to stop you, he can. Not because he's bigger, stronger, firmer, or even because he has a gun, but because he's authorized to act on the law's behalf. Exousia is the right to exercise kowach.

When Saint Paul says it was "the power which the Lord hath given me" (2 Corinthians 13:10 KJV), he was saying that the Christians in Corinth were under his God-given jurisdiction, and he wanted to exercise his spiritual authority appropriately. He was taking their circumstances, feelings, and knowledge into consideration. Great leaders skillfully exercise their power even in their absence. We've experience parents or partners, employees or associates who didn't consider our circumstances. They abused their power over us, making life more difficult than it had to be, as if life isn't already hard enough. One with this kind of power must be careful not to misuse it.

MIRACULOUS POWER

Another biblical Greek word for power is *dunamis*. We're familiar with dynamic and dynamite, they come from this word. It means energy or miraculous power. Dr. Strong says that in the Bible, "dunamis almost always points to new and higher forces that have entered and are working in this lower world of ours." You will know where God reigns because it will be characterized by His miraculous power to set things right. "For the kingdom of God is not in word, but in power" (1 Corinthians 4:20 NKJV). It's not shown in discussing, but in demonstrating, kingdom living is supposed to be dynamic in its demonstrations and as drastic as dynamite. Great lives have energetic, miraculous power from on high, awaiting the invasion of "this lower world of ours."

Dunamis is divine power that overcomes all resistance. In Jesus, it "resulted in dramatic transformation" (Strong's Concordance). This power is of the highest order; it cannot be resisted. When things don't work out for whatever reason—doctor's inaptitude, preacher's inability, or a partner's ignorance—you can still have a dramatic transformation.

Dramatic transformations characterized Saint Paul's ministry beginning with his conversion. He claimed that what Christ had accomplished through him was "in mighty signs and wonders, by the power of the Spirit of God, so that from Jerusalem and round about Illyricum I have fully preached the gospel of Christ" (Romans 15:19 NKJV). Signs are used to mark something; they point to someone or something other than themselves. Wonders are defined by "extraordinary occurrences, unusual manifestations; unexplainable phenomena" (Strong's Concordance). The *dunamis* of the spirit of God enabled him to heal the sick, cast out devils, and alter his environment for the glory of God. This was a mark of the miraculous that pointed to the existence of his God. It was also "extraordinary, unusual, and unexplainable." It pointed to the superiority of his God. God uses this power to transform things drastically! The apostle was convinced that if these transformations weren't happening in his ministry, he wasn't properly presenting the gospel. But with power, he confidently proclaimed, "I have fully preached the gospel of Christ" (Romans 15:19 NKJV). His gauge for preaching fully was that it had to be accomplished by signs and wonders. Can we say with him that we have "fully preached the gospel of Christ" or have we been afraid of stepping out in great faith to live with this aspect of greatness? His life's assignment could not be fulfilled without this *dunamis*. Many lives would have gone unchanged. Can you use this power in your present world? Do you or a loved one need a miracle? What about your future world? Are you going to need a fully preached gospel?

God's power gives you the ability to be forcefully firm (*kowach*), while standing in your authority (*exousia*), while being capable of the miraculous (*dunamis*). You can be solid, in command, and operate in the miraculous. The Bible calls it "great strength, and ability and power" (Acts 4:33 AMP).

GREAT POWER

The apostles prayed for boldness to minister. He gave it to them. "And with great power the apostles gave witness to the resurrection of the Lord Jesus. And great grace was on them all" (Acts 4: 33 NKJV). With substantial might, they made a case for Jesus being alive because they caused these miraculous transformations to happen in His name. Dead men don't have power, but the risen Savior does. With *dunamis*, the apostles blew up the works of the devil on a grand scale. Nobody else was having the impact on the world at that time that they were. They met and destroyed some of the major problems of their day, all kinds of sickness, diseases, demon possessions, and wrongful imprisonment.

The apostle Peter healed a man who was lame from his mother's womb. The man was looking for a financial handout which would have fed him but left him lame. Only great power would allow him to walk for the first time in his life. The apostle "took him by the right hand and lifted him up and immediately his feet and ankle bones received strength" (Acts 3:7 NKJV). One touch of this power from on high, and instantly his life was revitalized. The revitalization of your life could be one touch away! The unconquerable problems that we face today can be dissolved (corona, cancer, AIDs, famine, depression, and injustice). When doctors, exercise, nutrition, medicine, advisers, and lawyers fail you, you're still not at the mercy of the problem. Since the Father does not change or play favorites, whoever draws near to Him, like the apostles, can experience the same power they did. No, we don't all have apostolic authority (we won't be writing more books of the Bible), but we do have *exousia* authority. We can act on behalf of God as the apostles did. His greatness won't allow Him to shortchange us. Our generation will experience heaven's intervention in our regularly stressed lives. For God's significant, successful, satisfying power is still for His children's use.

A WITNESS

Power is great when it's of the highest quality and quantity. The Bible says, "The apostles gave witness to the resurrection of the Lord Jesus" (Acts 4:33 NKJV). When we think of someone being a witness, we picture someone testifying to something they have seen or heard.

They give their account or description of a person, place, or event. The Greek word used here for witness is *maturion*. It means "proof, evidence, and proclamation of personal experience." Its root is where we get our English word *martyr*, which is one who witnesses for Christ. Since so many of the first century witnesses gave their lives for Christ, a martyr became known as one who witnessed for Christ by dying for Him. Before the apostles' death, their witness wasn't just with the proclamation of words; they presented proof in the form of dramatic transformations that Jesus did, in fact, rise from the dead.

Their personal experience substantiated the resurrection of Christ. His great power had personally changed the course of their lives. They were some young crooks, tax extortioners, and fickle fishermen before Christ. The power of the once-dead Jesus had altered their lives. Now Jesus partnered with them to demonstrate some of the greatness of heaven through them.

A lawyer doesn't win his case in court because he's articulate with his words (he's not supposed to anyway). A lawyer wins his case because he can produce a witness or evidence that proves his argument is true. He has to have proof that his cause is justified. As attorneys for Jesus, the apostles went about making a case for the greatness of the risen Christ. Saint Paul's full preaching was witnessing because the signs and wonders that followed him was proof that what he was testifying of was real.

Who are you a witness for? What signs are following you? If I ask those around you, what would they say you're giving witness to? What do you complain about that you haven't allowed the miraculous power of God to change? Will you accept the responsibility of being a witness for him?

CAUTION

As a word of caution here, miracles working through you doesn't mean that all of your information or doctrine is true; it just means the one you're doing them for is real. God is true to His word that signs and wonders would follow His word. Satan is real also. He has "power, signs, and lying wonders" (2 Thessalonians 2:9 NKJV) that follow his believers because he is alive. Just as God has ambassadors in the earth fulfilling His will, Satan does too. When in doubt, listen for Jesus being lifted up, not a man or denomination. Great men want Jesus to get all the glory. The prideful want it all for themselves. Don't let a sign or wonder lie to you.

My desire is for this suffering world to have more encounters with wise biblical witnesses. I know there are people who have gone overboard with the supernatural; there are even charlatans who imitate the supernatural for personal gain. It doesn't nullify the authentic expression of God's power down here though; it only proves that it's real. No one imitates anything that hasn't first gotten some results. People only fake things that are real, things that are worth faking so the genuine serves as a template. You don't stop using $20 bills because counterfeit twenties exist. They wouldn't make you think that real twenties are not out there. No, you know that the counterfeits exist because the real twenties do. The counterfeit is actually evidence that there's a real thing.

Just as a $20 bill is for everybody to spend, this power is for all of God's children to dispense. It's not just for the apostle, prophet, evangelist, pastor, and teacher. The Bible says, "These signs will accompany those who believe: in my name they will drive out demons; they will speak in new tongues; they will pick up snakes with their hands; and when they drink deadly poison, it will not hurt them at all; they will place their hands on sick people, and they will get better" (Mark 16:17–18 NIV). We aren't to intentionally pick up snakes or drink any deadly poisons, but if we do, God's power released will nullify the effects of any sickness, disease, demons, language, or technological barrier. Any believer can witness. You can spend God's power here to purchase God's comfort and/or relief in this world's suffering.

WITNESS #1

JESUS'S WORKS

There's an old saying that goes, "Witness, witness, witness, and sometimes use words." I love that quote. It sums up what we've been discussing. Your life is testifying whether you know it or not. It's telling those around you that your God is all-powerful, or that He's not. That Jesus is alive, or He's not. Are people compelled to follow the God you serve? What is your life saying? Are you drawing a line in the sand?

Jesus drew that proverbial line in the sand. His character (love) and His conduct (power) distinguished Him from ordinary people; He stretched their comfort zone. He was busy witnessing for Father God.

Some of the Jews were doubting if Jesus was the foretold Messiah. They didn't discern His testimony. He enlightened them, "The very works that I do by the power of My Father and in My Father's name bear witness concerning Me [they are my credentials and evidence in support of Me]" (John 10:25 AMP). He pointed to the power that He used as evidence that He was the living Son of God. When He gave sight to the blind, He was saying nonverbally that He was the Christ. When He miraculously fed five thousand men and their families, He was saying that He was the Messiah. When He raised from the dead, He was saying that He was the Son of God. His accredited witness was His powerful works.

No minister performed the miracles that Jesus did while He was on earth. Yet from a prison cell, Jesus's cousin, John the Baptist, started to doubt Him. He was about to be beheaded, and since he was the opening act for Jesus's public ministry, surely Jesus would get him out of this. Wouldn't He? John sent a couple of his ministers to Him asking if He was the foretold Christ who was to come. "Jesus answered and said to them, 'Go and tell John the things which you hear and see; the blind see, and the lame walk; the lepers are cleansed, and the deaf hear; the dead are raised, and the poor have the gospel preached to them'" (Matthew 11:4–5 NKJV). He didn't answer them directly with,

"Yes, I am the Christ," or "No, I am not." The manifestations spoke for themselves. John knew that the Christ would have this great power, so when Jesus told of His authority and demonstrations, He was telling them that what He was doing was the evidence that He was the one to come. The number of miracles that Jesus performed was His exhibits A, B, and C. It was proof that He was the Christ.

The Lord pointed to the line that He drew for the world to see. After He told John's disciples about the signs following Him, He encouraged them "and blessed is he who is not offended because of Me" (Matthew 11:6 NKJV). He knew that he would stretch the faith of those around Him. If they resisted the temptation to be offended by His power, then they would be positioned to receive God's blessings. People are fickle, easy to be intimidated, and easily offended. If you push through that prideful tendency to feel inadequate, there's a blessing in it for you—happiness, joy, and rest. Who couldn't use more happiness, joy, and rest?

In the New Testament, no one provided as many opportunities to be offended as Jesus as no one had the quality nor the quantity of power that He did.

WITNESS #2
MOSES'S WORKS

Jesus had the direct line in the New Testament. In the Old Testament, it was Brother Moses who had it. No one was used as mightily as he was in the first covenant. He caused water to come from a rock miraculously at Rephidim. He caused the bitter waters to turn sweet at Morah so Israel could drink and live. He's best known for bringing the Israelites out of their Egyptian slavery. It's said of him that he "did all those miraculous signs and wonders the Lord sent him to do in Egypt—to Pharaoh and to all his officials and to his whole land. For no one has ever shown the mighty power or performed the awesome deeds that Moses did in the sight of all Israel" (Deuteronomy 34:11–12 NIV).

When Moses showed up in Egypt, it wasn't with persuasive words of wisdom. In fact, he took his brother, Aaron, with him to be the spokesman. He didn't go to witness with his words. He demanded the freedom of the Israelites, then he showed Pharaoh why he should let them go. There was blood in the Nile River. Frogs, lice, and flies infiltrated the land. The livestock of Egypt died. There were boils on the Egyptians, hail, swarms of locusts, thick darkness in all the land of Egypt for three days, and the death of all the firstborn. These ten plagues were Moses's witnessing tools (exhibits A to J) with which he testified to the greatness of the Lord.

You can imagine the massive line that was created through Moses's life. There were some in the camp that "grew envious of Moses" (Psalm 106:16 NIV). His life gave them cause to be offended. Excellence elicits envy. "The man, Moses, was very great in the land of Egypt, in the site of Pharaoh's servants and in the sight of the people" (Exodus 11:3 NKJV). The signs that followed him displayed his greatness while angering others, just like the Lord Jesus.

THE LORD AND THE PRINCE

Indeed, Saint Moses and the Lord Jesus were unsurpassed in their possession of great power. They were also unsurpassed in their perpetual humility vial setting. Moses wrote of himself, "Now Moses was a very humble man, more humble than anyone else on the face of the earth" (Numbers 12:3 NIV). Jesus said of Himself, "I am gentle and humble in heart" (Matthew 11:29 NIV). Yes, they said they were humble. It's not wrong to do so despite what we've been told. Remember, pride is not just arrogance; it's thinking too little of yourself. It's self-centeredness. Pride is a heart issue. If you're committed to the pie every day, then you can humbly proclaim your commitment. The right people will sense if you're genuine or not. I say all the time that

I'm endeavoring to be more humble every day. The problem is when prideful people think they're humble.

Our biblical power figures didn't have this problem. Moses grew up in Pharaoh's home, yet he, "when grown, refused the privileges of the Egyptian royal house. He chose a hard life with God's people" (Hebrew 11:24–25 MSG) so he could save his people, the Israelites. Moses dwelt among them. Jesus did the same. "He set aside the privileges of deity and took on the status of a slave, became human! Having become human, He stayed human. It was an incredibly humbling process" (Philippians 2:6–8 MSG). He did this so He could save his people, the entire world.

Moses was the closest to God while he was alive. He was the most intimate with him. To Aaron and Miriam, his brother and sister, God said, "If there is a prophet of God among you, I make myself known to him in dreams. But I don't do it that way with my servant Moses; he has the run of My entire house; I speak to him intimately" (Numbers 12:6–8 MSG). God kept the other prophets at bay, but not Moses. He allowed Moses to connect with Him deeply. Jesus was so close to the Father, He declared, "I and the Father are one, heart, and mind" (John 10:30 MSG). Jesus was perfectly synchronized with the Father's desires and methods. He and Moses exemplified the truth that the Father "brings the humble into fellowship with Him" (Psalm 138:6 MSG).

Moses was opposed by the most prideful man on earth at the time, Pharaoh. He saw himself as a god. What arrogance! Needless to say, he had the lowest perpetual humility vial setting in the land. God told Moses, "I'm sending you to Pharaoh to bring My people, the children of Israel, out of Egypt" (Exodus 3:10 MSG). Pharaoh held God's people captive until Moses arrived. Likewise, Jesus was opposed by the most prideful being, Satan. He tried to stop Jesus's ministry before it started by tempting Him to turn a stone into bread, throw Himself off the temple, and bow and worship him. In spite of those temptations, Jesus continued with His rescue, knowing that many are in "the devil's trap where they are caught and held captive" (2 Timothy 2:26 MSG), but Jesus came to set the captive free!

Satan tried to kill both Moses and Jesus as infants. "Pharaoh issued a general order to all his people: "Every boy that is born, drown him in the Nile" (Exodus 1:22 MSG). Moses could have been slain by that decree, but his mother hid him. Satan, through King Herod, "commanded the murder of every little boy two years old and under who lived in Bethlehem and its surrounding hills" (Matthew 2:16 MSG). Jesus would have been killed had his mother not taken him to Egypt. Satan knows what the humble can accomplish, so he's constantly on the attack. Note any kids who struggle with their imaginations or attention spans, their level of adversity in life is directly proportionate to their level of greatness. Satan doesn't want any more young Moses or Jesus rising up to destroy his works.

FASTING FOR THE GREAT

That's not all the Lord and the prince of Egypt had in common. They both fasted (abstained from foods) for forty days and forty nights. Fasting is an act of humbleness. King David knew the fastest way to discipline his flesh was to fast. He said, "[I] humbled myself with fasting" (Psalm 33:15 NIV). Fasting subdues the flesh; it produces drivenness, diplomacy, and detachability.

Going without food is an act contrary to the first act of sin— Adam and Eve partaking of the forbidden fruit. It's choosing to reject food in favor of fellowship with the Father. Doing so makes you closer to God than any other Christian discipline. When you die—if you're saved—you'll be as close to God as you can be (spirit to spirit). Fasting puts you as close to death as you can be on earth. You only have to go a few hours without food before your stomach starts growling. It will tell you, "You're going to die," "Feed me," or "I'm starving." It's an honor to tell God, "I choose Your belly over my belly. I want Your desires above my own." It's hard to be prideful when you're hungry. Adam and Eve made the wrong choice.

Fasting is tough. Americans weigh more today than ever before;

proof that we choose our bellies often. We eat a lot of junk food, chips, candy, and pies when we're celebrating and for comfort when we've lost. Consuming the wrong foods keeps us toxically hungry and craving nonnutritious, dead foods. Describing sinners, Saint Paul said, "Their god is their stomach (their appetites, their sensuality)" (Philippians 3:19 AMP). Today, people are doing whatever they have an appetite for (more food than we need, sex, drugs, and alcohol) while going without food is unthinkable to most. We lack the vision to foresee the benefits of it.

Yet there's no other way to have the kind of power that Jesus and Moses had than to fast, not eating at all (a total fast) or abstaining from certain kinds of foods (partial fasts). You can't stop watching TV or stop talking and call it a fast. There's no such thing as a fast from a bar, a club, or even bad thoughts. Bad thoughts should be eliminated from our lives altogether. To fast is to stop consuming physical food to feast on spiritual food. It's to deepen and enrich our relationship with the Father. The slight headaches and bad breath are worth the power that comes from proximity to God that fasting brings.

Fasting is beating hunger. If you can conquer your hunger, you'll have the power to conquer any storm. There's testimony after testimony of ordinary men and women who've participated in a three-day fast. I call it a resurrection fast. Just as Jesus got up from being dead in three days, in three days, their dead situations were resurrected. Direction followed, and great power was available. Power to change their world with clarity and contentment. I can testify of how it has brought me out of the darkness of depression. No surprise because the Bible promises that if we fast the way the Lord desires without complaining, conning, and catfighting, "then your light shall dawn in the darkness, and your darkness shall be as the noonday. The Lord will guide you continually, and satisfy your soul in drought, and strengthen your bones; you shall be like a watered garden, and like a spring of water, whose waters do not fail" (Isaiah 58:10–11 NKJV). See your relief from depression, your peace, your joy, direction, and power in there? "Your light shall dawn in the darkness," driving depression away. "The Lord will guide you continually" is your direction. The "satisfy your soul in drought and strengthen your bones; you shall be like a watered garden" is your peace and joy. Then to be "like a spring of water, whose waters do not fail" is your power.

If I could issue one challenge to the body of Christ, it would be to fast (drinking liquids only) for three days (seventy-two hours). The results will be nothing less than supernatural. The small mental lapse and lack of energy will pale in comparison to the benefits. You'll have a heightened sensitivity to the heart of God and the spirit realm. Immediately following the fast, your joy will increase. You'll be excited as you anticipate what the Father desires next. Your digestive system will be rejuvenated also because of the break.

You don't have to go forty days without food for great power. I've found that a three-day, liquids-only fast can connect you to the supernatural help. It's not easy, but it is worth it. Fasting will put you on God's short list like the Lord and Moses. When power is needed down here, God will call on you because you have consecrated yourself with fasting.

FASTING + PRAYER = POWER

After His forty-day fast in the desert, the Bible says that "Jesus returned to Galilee in the power of the Spirit and news about Him spread through the whole countryside" (Luke 4:14 NIV). His three-and-a-half-year ministry was birthed in power. He set an example; great *dunamis* comes on the other side of humbling yourself for usage through fasting and prayer. He emptied Himself of His own agenda. The pie empowered Him to detach from the world.

His forty-day fast provided Him with power for His three-and-a-half-year public ministry from the Feast of Tabernacles to His crucifixion on Passover. He is my example; so in like manner, I believe that no three-and-a-half-year period should go by in the life of the believer without fasting for at least forty days and forty nights. It doesn't have to be consecutive days. If you fast for one day a month over a three-and-a-half-year period, that would be forty-two days of humbling yourself. I like to use the three-day resurrection fast to accomplish this. Every three months or so, I kill the enemy of my flesh with a three-day feast on the things of God. That forty-two days makes you like Christ for three and a half years!Moses feasted on God for forty days too. It's no wonder Jesus used Moses's name while teaching more than any other Old Testament figure. Even more than the father of the faith, Abraham (Moses was mentioned twenty times, while Abraham was mentioned nineteen times). Jesus learned and quoted from the humble. Moses foretold the coming of the Lord Jesus, "The Lord your God will raise up for you a Prophet like me from your midst, from your brethren. Him you shall hear" (Deuteronomy 18:15 NKJV). Notice Jesus was to be "a" prophet (a minister) like Moses. He was to be of the same kind. He would be full of humble pie and not Himself like a lot of ministers today.

When Jesus taught on fasting, He didn't make it an option for His disciples. At the Sermon on the Mount, He said, "When you fast" (Matthew 6:16 NKJV), not "if you fast." He wanted us to be like Him, prepared to meet the problems of our day.

He also stated, "And when you pray" (Matthew 6:5 NKJV), not "if you want to or if you think it's a good idea." It's simply when you pray. Conversing with God is vital to walking in the anointing (the God ability). You must be willing to develop your prayer life. He wants to hear from His righteous children. You'll find that "the earnest (heartfelt, continued) prayer of a righteous man makes tremendous power available [dynamic in its working]" (James 5:16 AMP). Do you have the meekness to grasp the importance of prayer despite what your situation looks like?

I remember Bro. Reontae Robertson. He struggled mightily for a couple of years with an unknown sickness that caused his face to contort every ten seconds or so, forcing carbon dioxide from the side of his mouth like a horse. It was awful! While praying, he would hear voices in his head telling him that he wasn't praying to the real Jesus. He was under a persistent attack from Satan. His life began to disintegrate as his job performance fell behind his coworkers. He tried everything, even psych meds from his psychiatrist. Nothing worked! The

Lord put it on my heart to fast seven days (liquids only) for Brother Robertson's situation. I had never gone more than three days without eating. I had done multiple three-day fasts, but they were no easy feat. Yet I was keenly aware of what prayer and fasting could accomplish, and I wanted in on all that God wanted to do. I told another ministry friend, Min. Jake Bellamy, about the situation and found that God had put it on his heart to fast for a week as well. At the end of the fast, we met with Brother Reontae. It was a Wednesday night in the religious library at Lawrenceville Correctional Center. I'll never forget it. Minister Bellamy and I were standing behind a small table with our Bibles open. Brother Reontae was standing about ten feet away. We began the encounter with the Word. Minister Bellamy began calmly reading out loud from Mark 5 about Jesus casting out a legion of demons. As soon as the Word reached Reontae's ears, his legs gave away, and he dropped to the cold concrete floor. *Boom!* He started convulsing violently, not being touched by us but because he was in the presence of great power. Moving in the authority of the Word of God, we commenced to casting out all spirits and breaking any curses that might have been on him. We spoke healing and the blessing over that brother in love. Health and vitality were ushered in. Brother Reontae left that library completely delivered! That was almost seven years ago, and he is still delivered today. Prayer and fasting had brought relief where nothing else could. This was just confirming what Jesus said to be true; certain problems will persist unless there is "prayer and fasting" (Matthew 21:17 NKJV).

GREAT POWER STILL BELONGS TO THEM

Fasting and prayer is to accompany waiting patiently on the Lord. Before Jesus ascended into heaven, He told His disciples, "Behold, I send the Promise of My Father upon you; but tarry in the city of Jerusalem until you are ended with power from on high" (Luke 14:49 NKJV). He was referring to the day of Pentecost, which was less than two months away, when Holy Spirit would come and live in them as an internal power source like Jesus had in His ministry. Holy Spirit would be their divine enablement "from on high."

This initial endowment of power would mark the birth of the Church. He told more than five hundred of His followers to wait for Holy Spirit, but only 120 stayed put. Dynamic power was given to those who tarried in expectation, lingered in curiosity, and remained in unity. It was given to them who waited in obedience.

Today, great power still belongs to them who wait. Wait in prayer, wait in worship, wait in quietness before the Lord, wait in His Word. It is to them who set themselves apart from the world like on the day of Pentecost. There's no secret to the anointing. It rests with those who persevere. Will you wait on the Lord daily for firmness, authority, and the miraculous? The Bible says Moses, "Persevered because he saw Him who was invisible" (Hebrews 11:27 NIV). His commitment to God kept Him returning to His presence. He was one who waited.

I like to get alone with God and "come before His presence with singing" (Psalm 100:2 NKJV). He loves singing. It's a rhythmic right-hemisphere brain activity. It bypasses the logical left hemisphere producing harmonious adoration to the Father. I'm not much of a singer, but I like to say that He has perfect ears. So when the praises are released from my lips, they instantly reach His ears where He can interpret it as a perfectly pitched symphony! I've found that a lot of my alone time with Him turns into quiet time. After I open up in a song, I just wait there in His presence, soaking in the peace of that moment. I don't worry about my troubles. I'm engaged with the love of my life, Father God. From there, I expect to hear from Him in an audible voice, His inner audible voice, a vision, or an impression. Most of the time, I don't receive a direct word, but I do always find peace in His presence. I am a waiter.

It's interesting to note that the disciples didn't know what they were tarrying in Jerusalem for, nor did they know when it would come. They didn't know that the feast of Pentecost would alter their lives forever. Then "without warning there was a sound like a rushing wind, gale force – no one could tell where it came from. It filled the whole building. Then like a wildfire, the Holy Spirit spread through their ranks, and they started speaking in a number of different languages as the Spirit prompted them" (Acts 2:2–4 MSG). They had an experience with God. In the same way, we must keep waiting on God despite the uncertainty surrounding Him and His timing. We might not know how He's going to show up, but we can trust that He will show up.

Remember, they had waited for more than forty days with no experience, no sound, no feeling, no power. They were in Jerusalem, the place of their shame, where their Lord appeared to be defeated. Yet "when the Day of Pentecost had fully come" (Acts 2:1 NKJV), they were clothed with power from the risen Lord to effect change in their world. We must be confident enough in God to linger with Him privately despite any associated shame so we can change the world publicly.

Look at those used by the Lord today: Pastor Benny Hinn, Shawn Bolz, Randy Clark, Bill Johnson, Mahesh Chavda, Andrew Womack, Prophet Brian Carn, and many others all wait privately with the Lord. They led lives of consecration. Pastor Benny Hinn tells of when he was a young Christian, for one year straight, he would start around 8:00 p.m. and worship God until around 2:00 a.m. He knew he was nothing without the Lord. He's still a worshiper today. His waiting in worship on Humble Drive is inextricably connected to the power that has been filtered through him for over forty years!

POWER IN, POWER OUT

I'm not talking about being spooky; I'm talking about being supernatural. Christians are subject to all the trails and suffering that the world is. Yet God gives us the power to be firm and go through the storm or the authority and force to get out of it. Either way, God has us covered. We just have to trust God. He knows the type of power we need.

He wants us to "know and understand what is the immeasurable and unlimited and surpassing greatness of His power in and for us who believe, as demonstrated in the working of His mighty strength, which He exerted in Christ when He raised Him from the dead and seated Him at His [own] right hand in the heavenly [places]" (Eph. 1:19–20 AMP). God brought the Lord back from death, but He empowered Him to go through the storm of being killed. Power persevered Him through His execution, then power saved Him out of death.

There is immeasurable, unlimited, and unsurpassable grace for the children of God (great power to make His name great).

POWER FOR SICKNESS

Let's say you're driven, diplomatic, and detached enough to pray for someone who is sick, and it appears that nothing happens, what do you do? It's tough, but you persevere. You keep praying by faith in Jesus's name until you sense God calling it off. Don't let doubt and unbelief call it off. The humble's proximity to God allows him to pray for those that God wants to heal. Just like Jesus.

I like what Rabbi Jonathan Bernis tells the sick people that he prays for. He instructs them to confess that "when hands are laid on me, I will be healed." That's according to what Jesus told His disciples, that we would "place our hands on sick people and they will get well" (Mark 16:18 NIV). This builds the faith of those in need. I practice this often, resulting in signs and wonders following.

There are more ailments today than any other time in history. We need nutrients, exercise, and the best information from the medical field, but when they fail or have not been utilized, we need power from on high. God's power is available because God is ever concerned. We just have to be willing to step out in faith with this earth-shaken, burden-removing power!

Oh, that we would be able to say with the Apostle Paul, "I have strength for all things in Christ Who empowers me [I am ready for anything and equal to anything through Him Who infuses inner strength into me; I am self-sufficient in Christ's sufficiency]" (Philippians 4:13 AMP). Like the superpower America, I can enhance and improve what's around me through Christ's sufficiency.

YOUR PIECE OF THE PIE:
GREAT LEADERSHIP

You've observed how godless rulers throw their weight around, how quickly a little power goes to their heads. It's not going to be that way with you. Whoever wants to be great must become a servant

.—Matthew 20:25–26 (MSG)

It was the beginning of my seventh-grade school year. I was twelve years old, 130 pounds, about five feet and five inches, athletic, and a pretty good basketball player. My custom was to come home and change into my play clothes to shoot some hoops in the backyard or on our dirt basketball court by myself, most days. This particular day wasn't like most. This day my only brother, William Wilson Jr., came down to embarrass me with his superior ball-playing abilities in a one-on-one game. He was seventeen years old, 170 pounds, and about six feet and two inches. He was bigger, stronger, and taller than me, a junior in high school, and a member of the varsity basketball team. Despite my love for the game, he had no intentions of letting me win. It was his time to shine! We started playing my ball first. My jump shot kept the score close, but then my brother turned it up. He was playing like it was game seven of the NBA finals. It was as if he was commissioned to make me feel as awful as possible. My ego got smaller and smaller as he scored over and over again, almost effortlessly. It was like Stephen Curry against Kevin Hart!

After losing a couple of games, I stood there with my hands on my head, sweating profusely, grasping for air, and digging deep for the strength to continue. My pride wouldn't let me tap out, no matter how bad I felt physically and emotionally. Just then, I looked up, and coming toward us was my next-door neighbor's grandson. He was a ninth grader, about five feet and nine inches, 150 pounds, and a fairly skilled basketball player. He had no desire to play; he was just coming by to speak. Quietly, I analyzed the situation and told my brother that he couldn't beat me and my friend at the same time. Embracing the stardom of the moment, my brother exclaimed, "He can get it too!" Feeling the intensity on the court, my friend asked me what was going on. Looking as dejected as I could, I told him something to the effect of, "I'm in trouble and I need help; he can't beat both of us." He tied his tennis shoes tight and put his game face on.

It was a challenge my brother couldn't refuse. All we had to do was score twelve baskets before he did. We played hard, taking advantage of ball movement to neutralize my brother's size. It was touch-and-go for a while, but in the end, we prevailed.

Now I didn't expect my friend to show up that day, so I wasn't expecting to beat my brother. After one game, we quit, even though my brother wanted to get us back. He was going to leave there with nothing but the taste of defeat. As we headed to the house, we taunted him with celebratory laughs, victory jumps, and fist pumps! He was so mad he picked my fifteen-speed bicycle up and fiercely slammed it to the ground. *Boom!* It was the agony of defeat!

It was a memorable day. I had accomplished with my friend what I could not have on my own. That's what leadership is—awakening a desire in others to help you accomplish what you could not accomplish sensibly on your own. It's being able to communicate a clear objective and plan to achieve it with clarity. That day would've been like all the other days before it if good leadership (convincing my friend to join me) wasn't there to bring all the ingredients together for a win.

THE HEAD OF THINGS

Leadership is the act of leading. It's your ability to engage and rally others. It's the degree to which you impact others. It's also your ability to convey information. It describes the atmosphere you set and the total influence you have. It is essential for everything that involves people.

While giving instructions, Moses told the Israelites to "make captains of the armies to lead the people: (Deuteronomy 20:9 NKJV). This Hebrew word for lead is *rosh*. Dr. Strong uses words like "chief, head, top, first, sum, point, and beginning" to describe it. Moses sought out leaders to be chief in their commitment, at the top of obligation, first in responsibility, able to represent the sum of the talent that they're over, and those at the point or beginning of accountability. That's what leadership is, being chiefly accountable.

Rosh depicts leading at the front. It's what comes down or what's hooked to for assistance because it's the highest in rank, the governing position. Discerning and delegation happens here. Rosh is the starting point. It heads up all things.

Moses's leaders were needed to help him accomplish what he could not accomplish without them. They were to rally the troops, bring out their potential, and filter down information. The organization of the Israelites was imperative because their army would be outnumbered at every battle they fought. Ineffective leadership would have destroyed them. In his book, *Leadership Gold*, John Maxwell quotes Lee Robertson as saying, "Everything rises and falls on leadership" because leadership is at the head of all things. When the head is right, the body will follow. The head is always making things better or worse for the body. It's never neutral.

That is why the Bible says of the body of Christ, the Church, that "the gates of Hades shall not prevail against it" (Matthew 16:18 NKJV). Jesus is the head of the Church, leading out front. The Church is triumphant no matter how bad it looks. She will win in the end. She will excel at the right things, at the right places, and at the right times, for her leader has risen! The gospel will be preached, souls will be saved, bodies will be healed, and lives will be blessed and forever changed. The Church will rise because its head, Jesus, rose. Where the head goes, the body follows. Where the tip of the spear goes, the body of the spear follows. If the pointy end hits its target, then the body does too. There's no disconnect, for the body rest in the headship of the point. The only question is, are you a part of the body? If you are, then His will for you, your family, your career, and church will be done!

A GUIDE

There's another Hebrew word for lead. Jacob used it when he told his brother, Esau, "I will lead on slowly at a pace which the livestock that go before me, and the children are able to endure" (Genesis 33:14 NKJV). The word is *nahal*. Dr. Strong depicts it as a "flow, hence to conduct and to protect, sustain; carry, feed, guide, lead (gently on)." Like a lazy river, Brother Jacob was going to gently lead, guide, feed, sustain, and protect the children and livestock under his care. He considered the needs of the weakest among them and decided how he was going to care for them. "Leadership gains authority and respect when the voiceless poor are treated fairly" (Prov. 29:14 MSG). Jacob was respected by the families he was leading. They followed his *nahal*. *Nahal* is capable leadership. It's systematically stimulating yourself and inspiring others to do the same.

People want to follow one who is sure of where they're going and how to get there. There's no substitute for competent capability. I'm not talking about being a rocket scientist but being able to deal with the pressure and people in your position wisely. You should be willing to learn all you can about your position and those above and beneath you.

Brother Jacob was saying that he knew where he was going and how he was going to get himself and his feeble followers there. His pace was determined by his pupils. In the same way, the pace of leadership in your family, community, corporation, and church should be determined by the ability of those you are leading. You must perpetually adjust to the personalities, problems, and potential of the people following you.

Knowing the personalities, problems, and potential of two young fishermen, Jesus implored them, "Follow Me, and I will make you fishers of men. They immediately left their nets and followed Him" (Matthew 4:19–20 NKJV). Peter and Andrew had met Jesus earlier, and now because of His competence, they left their craft to switch careers at His word. They wanted Jesus to be responsible for them. His leadership compelled them to follow. Leadership is looking back and seeing people wanting your guidance because your level of understanding in a particular area exceeds theirs. "The mark of a good leader is loyal followers, leadership is nothing without a following" (Prov. 14:28 MSG).

A HEAD GUIDE

"When the country is in chaos everybody has a plan to fix it—but it takes a leader of real understanding to straighten things out" (Proverbs 28:2 MSG). It's competent, diligent leaders who excel at problem-solving. God wants us to increase our understanding so we can "straighten things out" in the earth. He's looking for capable leadership to arise.

We've all been under leadership that wasn't as informed or capable as it should have been. As a result, there was some kind of abuse of friends, followers, or finances. Corruption was inevitable. That's because the Bible says, "Among leaders who lack insight, abuse abounds, but for one who hates corruption, the future is bright" (Proverbs 28:1 MSG). To brighten things up, leadership has to be bright enough to despise corruption.

God is looking for some head guides. He wants men and women to head up the guidance in the earth. Guidance in righteousness, guidance in holiness, guidance in justice, guidance in true prosperity and the things of God. He wants competent, diligent guides to listen, learn, lift, and lead; that's leadership.

THE 4 LS OF LEADERSHIP

Listen. Saint James said to "post this at all the intersections, Dear friends: lead with your ears, follow up with your tongue" (James 1:19 MSG). Brother James wanted us all to be better listeners. He wanted us to detach from everything else in and around us and hear what's bothering people. If you listen long enough, they'll tell you. People want to be around good listeners. Before anything, we have to listen first in all of our encounters. This one key applied would make many leaders greater.

Learn. Brother Titus said, "Let our people also learn to maintain good works, to meet urgent needs that they may not be unfruitful" (Titus 3:14 NKJV). To stay fruitful, we must be driven to learn. Important and urgent needs change all the time, so a good work yesterday may not necessarily be a good work today. Giving me a book to help me today may be good, but tomorrow a book may be an insult to my situation. We have to learn to maintain good works.

Lift. Words that build others up are always welcomed. Saint Paul says to "speak encouraging words to one another. Build up hope so you'll all be together in this, no one left out, no one left behind" (1 Thessalonians 5:11 MSG). Encouragement is so underrated. God knows that we all need it. He made us to receive and give uplifting words as temporary refreshments. We all need to be infused with hope, not flattery but genuine optimistic assessments. People won't turn that kind of lift down.

Lead. After listening, learning, and lifting, you'll be known, liked, and respected by more people. You'll have earned the right to lead them, to be their chief guide. Jesus called the Pharisees "blind guides" (Matthew 23:16 NKJV). They had no desire to embrace other people's worlds; they only wanted to look good in front of them. They didn't listen to, learn from, or lift up those who needed them most. Jesus said, "Forget them. They are blind men leading blind men. When a blind man leads a blind man, they both end up in the ditch" (Matthew 5:14 MSG). To lead is to see a path and a people and to know what to do with both. The Pharisees were awful leaders who didn't "speak encouraging words" to many; they were known for their condemnation. They didn't "learn to maintain good works;" they only learned God's law. They certainly didn't "lead with their ears;" they liked listening to themselves! How easy it is for us to be like those Pharisees. In fact, without humble pie, we are those Pharisees. Our words may be different, but our thoughts will be the same as theirs. You're either leading from pride or from the pie. If it's from pride, then you'll fail with the four Ls of leadership. Like the Pharisees, a few people will benefit, and a lot of people will be sorrowed.

STELLAR LEADERSHIP

Great leadership then is being an excellent head guide, a great listener, a great learner, a great lifter, and a great leader. It's being proficient in every position you hold. As a parent, employee, or an entrepreneur, you need superb leadership qualities. You're a leader who is pursuing a great life, a great mind, great faith, a great vision, great power, and great relationships.

A great life is needed because the leader needs to be close to God to get His marching orders. Biblically, "good leadership is a channel of water controlled by God; He directs it to whatever end He chooses" (Proverbs 21:1 MSG). God doesn't make bad choices. The question is, am I willing to pursue Him to be in the center of His will for me and those following me?

A great mind is needed too. A great leader will face great intellectual challenges. He has to be well-rounded and able to develop his followers. He has to challenge them to get error out of the camp. "Like the horizons for breadth and the ocean for depth, the understanding of a good leader is broad and deep" (Proverbs 25:3 MSG). A broad and deep understanding of yourself and your team breeds longevity in leadership.

Great faith will be needed as well. There will be obstacles in front of you and your team (bills, divisions, immorality, etc.), and faith in God will get you through it peacefully. Your team has to know that you trust God for your results. A great leader communicates his dependence on God regularly. They know they need God more, not less, as they grow. After describing some of His suffering for Christ, Saint Paul said, "Instead of trusting in our own strength or wits to get out of it, we were forced to trust God totally—not a bad idea since He's the

God who raises the dead" (2 Corinthians 1:9 MSG)! The apostle was saying if He can raise the dead, then certainly obstacles are no match for Him. God has designed it so that through our faith in Him, we can do great things, and as a result, He will get the glory.

A great vision is needed to take you and your team from where you are to where God wants you to be. With your purpose (why you exist) and your mission (how you'll fulfill your purpose) in place, your vision will empower your team to excel. A great vision attracts followers and sets parameters on your activity. Any activity or person that doesn't aid in achieving the vision you eliminate, that is detach from it. "After careful scrutiny a wise leader makes a clean sweep of rebels and dolts" (Proverbs 20:26 MSG). It's wise to get the pride out. To permit any rebellion or incompetence is to approve of it, but "good leaders abhor wrongdoing of all kinds; sound leadership has a moral foundation" (Proverbs 16:12 MSG). A small crack can sink a boat; get and keep error out. A leading vision will expose all insubordination, stupidity, and immorality.

Great power will be needed at some point as well. A great leader needs to stand firm in his authority and have God's power working through him to overcome all opposition to the vision. Your team will trust and want to help a powerful leader. The same goes for a powerful speaker, people person, administrator, prayer warrior, faith healer, or miracle worker. The more powerful things God does through you, the more He's glorified, and the more people are going to follow you. God "is able to do immeasurably more than all we ask or imagine, according to His power that is at work within us" (Ephesians 3:20 NIV).

Finally, great relationships are essential for this level of leading. Nothing great is achieved without the help of others. Everyone has their own area of expertise. "Many hands make light work" is the old saying. Many mistakes will be avoided, much time will be saved, and more will be produced when great relationships are in place. Potential will be tapped into, and others will be helped as the vision begins to come to pass. Great relationships allow us to know more than we've learned and see more than what our eyes have beheld. It is the right people around a leader who increases his value and subsequent impact. "God loves the pure hearted and well-spoken; good leaders also delight in their friendship" (Proverbs 22:11 MSG). Like God, great leaders value the abilities of others. They diplomatically draft them to the team. "Observe people who are good at their work – skilled workers always in demand and admired; they don't have a backseat to anyone" (Proverbs 22:29 MSG). Great leaders discover, develop, and deepen great relationships with skilled followers and other leaders.

A ONE-WAY ROAD

It's clear then that the pie makes a leader great. Pride is so distasteful. The Bible says, "By pride comes nothing but strife, but with the well-advanced is wisdom" (Proverbs 13:10 NKJV). Not by pride comes strife sometimes, no, "by pride comes nothing but strife." It's a one-way round. That's exhaustive language; pride produces strife. If you have a strife problem, it's because you have a pride problem. When pride shows up in some form, discord shows up too. When trouble shows up, it's because humility has left. Adam and Eve would have lived on without knowing trouble, if Eve would have never given place to pride. She was tempted by the desire to be like God. They both ate the forbidden fruit, and strife was erected between them and God.

Pride destroyed the relationship they had with the Father because the advice of wisdom was disregarded. Oh, if Adam had been a great leader at that moment, he would have:

- listened to Eve's dilemma;
- learned of her desires;
- lifted her perspective; and then
- led her right out of that error.

PRIDE OUT, REVIVAL IN

Pride is deadly. The cities of Sodom and Gomorrah were destroyed with a rain of fire and brimstone. Everything that grew from the ground and everyone in it, except Lot and his children, was wiped away. Only smoke remained in those cities after their destruction. God annihilated them because they "had pride" (Ezekiel 16:49 NKJV). In their haughtiness, they did whatever it was that brought them immediate gratification—fornication, adultery, homosexuality, and the like.

God was tired of them being their own god. They ignored Him, so He briefly ignored them. He didn't intervene, so they were wiped away by a meteor shower.

Pride will bring your team down just like these cities. Rebuking the Israelites' pride, Isaiah cried, "Listen to my message, you Sodom schooled leaders. Receive God's revelation you Gomorrah – schooled people" (Isaiah 1:10 MSG). Isaiah's message to them was to humble themselves. Their leaders were prideful just like the inhabitants of Sodom and Gomorrah, and the people were a reflection of them. It's not hard for leaders to fall into pride like Nebuchadnezzar. Being over people can cause us to exalt ourselves when it should be others who exalt, encourage, and appreciate us. God wanted Israel's leaders to humble themselves and lead His people into repentance in order to revive them, but they were victims of the central evil—pride.

The pie has always been the prerequisite to revival. God's decree is, "If My people who are called by My name will humble themselves, and pray, seek My face, and turn from their wicked ways, then I will hear from heaven, and will forgive their sin and heal their land" (2 Chronicles 7:14 MSG). God wants to speak from heaven, forgive sins, and heal situations in the land, including the land itself. It's pride that's stopping Him. America can be healed. God gave us the formula; it's no secret. We have to get on Humility Avenue. We won't be heard until we get there. A great awakening will not occur until we get there.

PRIDE IS EXPENSIVE

While Rehoboam was king in Judah, the people had abandoned God. Like many people today, God wasn't important to them. So God let Shishak, king of Egypt, invade Israel and the cities of Judah. Now King Shishak was closing in on Israel's capital, Jerusalem. It was a cavalry of sixty thousand horsemen and twelve hundred chariots. King Rehoboam and the leaders of Israel had retreated to Jerusalem. There, the prophet Shemaiah told them the Lord said, "You have abandoned Me, so I am abandoning you to Shishak" (2 Chronicles 12:5 NLT). Without the Lord's protection, Jerusalem was like Sodom and Gomorrah, on the brink of destruction.

"Then the leaders of Israel and the king humbled themselves and said, 'The Lord is right in doing this to us'" (2 Chronicles 12:6 NLT)! They realized that it was their evil pride that was bringing this calamity on them. They took God's formula and got on the right road. Then God spoke from heaven, "When the Lord saw their change of heart, He gave this message to Shemaiah: 'Since the people have humbled themselves, I will not completely destroy them and will soon give them some relief. I will not use Shishak to pour out my anger on Jerusalem'" (2 Chronicles 12:7 NLT). The Lord made it clear that their destruction was stopped because their pride had stopped. It was an act of greatness; the leaders had saved their people by leading them into the place of humility.

Now King Shishak still attacked Jerusalem. He raided Rehoboam's palace and the Lord's temple. He took everything he could, including all the fold furnishings that King Solomon had made. Then he went on about his business. Jerusalem was not destroyed, but staying in pride cost them. Had they humbled themselves earlier, they may not have lost as much. Sometimes we stay in pride too long, and like any sin, we end up paying more than we expected. Every minute we're in pride, it costs us. It's not a question of if it will cost us; the only question is how much it will cost us. We love to hold on to our pride until we see the effects of it. It took Rehoboam's kingdom to be faced with annihilation for him to repent.

What is your pride costing you and your team? Will you have a culture that travels on Humility Avenue (the road that all obedience is fulfilled)? What area of your organization is infested with pride? What is it costing your finances, your influence, your energy, and your health? Pride is expensive!

SACRIFICE

Another aspect of great leadership is making great sacrifices. Sound leaders make sound sacrifices. The strength of a leader is directly proportionate to the sacrifices he makes. The Bible says of Jesus, "And being found in appearance as a man, He humbled Himself and became obedient to the point of death, even the death of the cross" (Philippians 2:8 NKJV). The greatest leader (Jesus) made the greatest sacrifice (death) so that His followers might have eternal life. He "appeared to put away sin by the sacrifice of Himself" (Hebrews 9:16 NKJV). That was His assignment. He did what His followers could not—sacrifice Himself for their salvation.

Sound leadership will sacrifice whenever, whatever, and whoever they need to for God and their organization. It may mean more time in the prayer closet, at the office, or even at home. It could mean more education or more vacation. The driven, diplomatic, and detachable leader will give up what he has to and take on what may be uncomfortable for the betterment of the team.

Your contribution has to be significant. Your sacrifice has to display your discipline. You have to be satisfied with the decision. What drive, diplomacy, and detachability Jesus must have had to offer Himself up to be slain when He could have prevented it. He knew that preventing it would have destroyed His movement. The right sacrifice will produce longevity for you and your followers.

Examine your team. What sacrifice do you need to make? What department needs more resources? What person needs more training?

Who doesn't understand the vision? How can you give more of yourself for the cause? Every day you wake up, remember that great leaders make great sacrifices. Like Jesus, you must embrace the discomfort of today in order to bring forth the vision of tomorrow. I know being brutally beaten and crucified wasn't comfortable, but that's what Jesus's position called for, for maximum impact. What sacrifice does your position require of you to have maximum impact?

SERVANT LEADERSHIP

The leader makes great sacrifices because he's a great servant. Jesus warned His followers about the leaders of their day. "You've observed how godless rulers throw their weight around, how quickly a little power goes to their heads. It's not going to be that way with you. Whoever wants to be great must become a servant" (Matthew 20:25–26 MSG). These rulers were prideful and important (in their own minds) because they had a position; they were recognized leaders. They wanted all the servants they could get. The more you had, the more important or greater you were deemed to be. Jesus taught that to be great was to be sure of yourself enough to take the position of a servant. Greatness is measured by service, not by the number of servants you have.

Biblically, a servant was the lowest social designation you could have. They did what most people considered beneath them to do, like wash feet, clean rooms and clothes, and assist others in any menial task they may have. Anybody could be a servant. There was no certification or extensive training course. If you couldn't do anything else, you know you could be a servant. Jesus saved the world as a servant. He said, "He came to serve, not be served—and then to give away His life in exchange for the many who are held hostage" (Matthew 20:28 MSG). He was a pleasant servant to His followers during His public ministry. He even washed His twelve disciples' feet. But His greatest act of service was sentencing Himself to a thirty-three-and-a-half-year human prison sentence and giving away His life in exchange for us, the real prisoners! Every moment of His life was a gift to humanity.

As the authority on giving service, Jesus posed a question to His disciples, "Do you want to stand out? Then step down. Be a servant. If you puff yourself up, you'll get the wind knocked out of you. But, if you're content to simply be yourself, your life will count for plenty" (Matthew 23:11–12 MSG). Serve with and through your personality, whether you're an introvert (phlegmatic or melancholy), extrovert (sanguine or choleric), or an ambivert (introverted and extroverted).

Be among the people. Don't micromanage, but trust and be aware of where you're needed. Servants don't force their way into situations; room is always made for them. Their life counts for plenty because they don't mind stooping down to give assistance.

Like Jesus, the humble leader doesn't discriminate in his service. He gives frequently and voluntarily. The great leader, Saint Paul said, "Even though I am free of the demands and expectations of everyone, I have voluntarily become a servant to any and all in order to reach a wide range of people" (1 Corinthians 9:19 MSG). The apostle served people genuinely even though he wasn't obligated to. The love of God had conditioned his heart to care for people. To be an effective servant, you have to genuinely care for people.

Saint Paul had followers from all walks of life; he served them on their terms, explaining, "I entered their world and tried to experience things from their point of view. I've become just about every sort of servant there is in my attempts to lead those I meet into a God-saved life" (1 Corinthians 9:22 MSG). He met people where they were and excelled at serving. Is there any service you can excel at?

LEAD YOURSELF

A great leader listens, learns, lifts, and leads him or herself. They are heaven leaders, not earth leaders. "Earth leaders push for position"

(Psalm 2:2 MSG). You'll be tempted to exaggerate, manipulate, undermine, and downright lie to be in a good position. That's why the first person you have to lead is yourself. Where are you prone to mess up at? Is it a love for money, lust for men or women, covetousness for a title or position? By the grace of God, you can overcome any personal defect. I don't care how long you or your team have had it. After you've overcome, guard your weakness in character and ability. Have clear guidelines. Have someone other than yourself sign off on all financial decisions. Don't lose sight of who you are. A title won't make you any more valuable to God than you are now. Make sure the people around you hold you accountable. Jesus said, "Woe to you when all men speak well of you" (Luke 6:26 NKJV). Beware when everybody's agreeing with you. If everyone's agreeing with you, then no new ideas are birthed, and you aren't being held accountable.

TRUST GOD

In all things, trust God. He wants you to be a great leader for a great people like I was the day my friend and I beat my brother in basketball. God brought the victory. When you're driven to Him every day, you'll be sensitive to how and when to be diplomatic with people, that is when to listen, learn, lift, and lead. You're going to be required to pivot often, to read people and plans, and to know what to do in a moment's time. God will lead you to detach from dated people and plans. Just trust Him.

YOUR PIECE OF THE PIE:
GREAT WEALTH

There was a relative of Naomi's husband, a man of great wealth,
of the family Elimelech. His name was Boaz.

—Ruth 2:1 (NKJV)

Soon as I was big enough to ride a bike without training wheels, I was hooked. I would ride almost every afternoon up and down our residential street. The neighbors on our street with paved driveways would allow the neighborhood kids to ride their bikes around them. Or maybe we just did that when they weren't home! Either way, one day after school, a few of us were riding around as usual. I was about six years old, just old enough to be out there with the bigger kids. I remember riding a bike that was slightly bigger than a kid my size should be ridding. There were four of us playing outside like kids did back in the early '90s.

My grandmother's modest abode was next door to ours. We were riding around her horseshoe driveway when I turned my handlebars too sharply and was thrown violently to the concrete. *Boom!*

I looked at the abrasion on the side of my left arm and started crying. I wanted my mama! I held my arm close to my chest and cried all the way home. Through watery eyes, I told my mama about the crash, and that I couldn't bend my arm. I thought it was broken. I never broke anything before, so I thought this was it. We jumped in our blue minivan and rushed to the emergency room. On the way to the hospital, I realized that my condition wasn't that serious, and I didn't need a doctor, but we were already committed to getting me to Martinsville Memorial Hospital. So I kept the tears coming.

After waiting for a while, I was summoned from the waiting room. The nurse examined and prepared me for an X-ray. It was then that she concluded that it wasn't a break; it was just a close call. You see, my strawberry scrape was right on my elbow, making it hard but not impossible for me to bend. I'll never forget the look of disdain that my mother gave me. I turned away, but her stare had already spoken. "I know you didn't cost me whatever this deductible is going to be for a little scrape on your arm!"

WEALTH NEEDED

Though she never said it, my mom looked at me like that because we weren't wealthy. We were not poor, but we didn't have emergency money for an emergency room trip.

I know now that that's not God's best for His children, and that many of His children don't have enough wealth to cover family emergencies or any unexpected expense. You hear so much about money and prosperity today that I don't like teaching on it. I've heard hundreds of sermons on wealth and financial literacy. I guess it's fatigue.

Yet I am keenly aware that if the money problem in most homes were solved, then peace would come to that home. Solve the money problem in most companies, churches, communities, cities, and counties, and most of the fighting would cease. The stress that's harmful to your body and is affecting your quality of life would be avoided. Families would be saved, and businesses would have longevity. I want everyone to know about God's plan for their money.

I heard Pastor Benny Hinn say it like this, "Money is not the most important thing in the world, but it effects the most important things in your world." The Bible is clear, "Laughter and bread go together, and wine gives sparkle to life—but it's money that makes the world go around" (Ecclesiastes 10:19 MSG). To have the significance, success, and satisfaction God wants to give us, wealth is required.

ENOUGH

What is wealth then? King Solomon said that "wealth attracts friends as honey draws flies, but poor people are avoided like a plague" (Proverbs 19:4 MSG). The Hebrew word there for wealth is *hown*. Dr. Strong describes it as "Substance, riches, possessions, and enough. It usually refers to movable goods. It can represent any kind of concrete wealth," anything that you can own that someone considers valuable, something you can buy or barter with. It's having enough possessions, riches, or substance to take care of your needs and someone who's worse off than you are. King Solomon was sighting how people are drawn to people who they consider rich like, flies to honey. We are interested in what wealthy people are doing, what kind of house they have, cars they drive, and the clothes they wear. Yet the poor are avoided because their needs aren't met. They have no movable goods or concrete wealth that's desirable.

Hown is prospering in your pocketbook. It's not ungodly to have or want money. You just cannot be consumed by its attainment as billions of people are today. Money, in itself, is not evil, but to constantly crave it (to lust after it) is evil because you were made to constantly crave the Creator. He wants to sit on the throne of our hearts in place of our material things.

"The love of money is the root of all kinds of evil. And some people, craving money, have wandered from the true faith and pierced themselves with many sorrows" (1 Timothy 6:10 NLT). The reason so many are hurting today is because they are disproportionately desiring money. When they don't get the material things that they see everybody else with, disappointment, discouragement, and depression ensue.

Having things doesn't hurt anyone, but loving them does. It's up to us what we fall in love with. It's tough because we are prone to fall in love with what we spend time with. We are around material things and use or think about using money every day. Yet God wants us to keep the appropriate relationship with it and Him.

He doesn't want us to worship wealth as if it were a god. Jesus said it like this, "You can't worship two gods at once. Loving one god, you'll end up hating the other. Adoration of one feeds contempt for the other. You can't worship God and money both" (Matthew 6:24 MSG). You don't have to choose between God and money; you just have to choose which one you are going to worship. God is to be worshiped with money; you can't use God to worship money.

People pay homage to money because they think it will give them what only God can, security and stability. How many people do you know that if they had a little more money, they would be safe and situated? Money does give you more options, but only God can provide lasting safety and stability so He's the only one worthy of worship. To know which one you've been worshiping, examine the decisions you've made in the last thirty days. Did you compromise in some way to benefit your bottom line?

CAPABLE OF CREATING

There's another Hebrew word for wealth called *chayil*. Dr. Strong found it to mean "strength, power, wealth, property, capable, valiant, army, troops, influential, upper class people." This word signifies a faculty or power, the ability to effect or produce something." It's being capable of generating income.

The sons of Korah used the word *chayil* when they observed that there are "those who trust in their wealth [chayil] and boast in the multitude of their riches" (Psalm 49:6 NKJV). They noticed that most rich people rest in the safety that riches provide and in their ability to get more riches. They worship around their faculty or power to effect and produce money. They've experienced what money has made happen for them, but they don't resist the temptation to fall in love with it and their ability to produce it.

Chayil is being influential because you bring about finances.

When you have this, you're never poor regardless of what your bank statements and liabilities say. You're always wealthy because even if you lose money, you still retain the ability to get it. The Bible says that Boaz was "wealthy and influential" (Ruth 2:1 NLT). President Trump is wealthy and influential. He has lost significant amounts of money a few times, but he's always gotten it back and then some. No one would doubt Warren Buffet or Bill Gates's ability to do the same thing. That's *chayil*.

Again, having wealth and being capable of creating it with integrity is not bad. Money just magnifies who you are. If you indulge in drinking or pornography, then with more money, you would drink more alcohol and watch more pornography. If you take care of your family without any bad habits, then with wealth, you'll be able to do it a little better. Who and what you spend your money on is a representation of who you are. You cannot hide who you are. Look at your checkbook, your credit card statements, your credit score. They are pictures of what a person like you does. Where you spend your money reveals your heart. Jesus said it like this, "Wherever your treasure is, there the desires of your heart will also be" (Matthew 6:21 NLT). You want to know if your desires align with God's? Track where your money is going.

This is why we discussed having a rich relationship with God and investing in a connection with Him. It's so you can view money and material things as He does, tools to fulfill His will. The more of it you have, the more people you can feed, educate, heal, and rescue. Not having it shrinks your influence. It mutes your voice. Poverty is not cute nor is it biblical. It's actually selfish. Without wealth, you'll suffer, and those you could have helped with wealth will stay in the trouble which you could have alleviated if you were wealthy.

A LOT OF MONEY

Being wealthy then is not getting a big check on the first and the fifteenth and owing it out because you're living beyond your means. Or maybe you're living within your means and your family is taken care of, but your ends are barely meeting, so you have nothing to give. Being wealthy is not just having a lot of money at some point in the year as most lottery winners would attest to. Many big prize winners end up broke shortly after winning because although they got a lot of money, they never got real wealth, enough money and the ability to get more of it.

Father Abraham had real wealth, both *hown* and *chayil*. His servant said of him, "The Lord has blessed my master abundantly and he has become wealthy. He has given him sheep and cattle, silver and gold, menservants and maidservants, and camels and donkeys" (Genesis 24:35 NIV). The Lord had blessed him indeed. They didn't have the luxurious standards we have today, but he had the equivalent. The best in travel (camels and donkeys) and the best in livestock (sheep and cattle). When he died, he was buried in land that he had purchased with his blessings. He had what he needed to fulfill the call of God on his life, enough money and the ability to get more of it.

HUGE WEALTH FOR HUGE ASSIGNMENT

Boaz was "a man of great wealth, of the family Elimelech" (Ruth 2:1 NKJV). He came from a pretty well-to-do family which may have passed down some of his huge wealth. In one of his fields of grain, a Moabite widow named Ruth was gleaning the grain that Boaz had his servants leave on purpose. His possessions (the grain) met a need of hers (hunger). The two hit it off. Soon, "Boaz married Ruth. She became his wife. Boaz slept with her. By God's gracious gift she conceived and had a son" (Ruth 4:13 MSG). Their son's name was Obed. He was the grandfather of King David and an ancestor of the Lord Jesus. Brother Boaz had the huge assignment of being in the genealogy that would bring forth the Savior of the world!

Brother Job had a few assets. He owned seven thousand sheep, three thousand camels, five hundred yoke of oxen, and five hundred donkeys, and a large number of servants. He was the greatest man among all the people of the east (Job 1:2–3 NIV). He was the richest man in his country. Unlike Boaz, there's no formal introduction of his family line which suggests that he may have gotten his great wealth all on his own. He seems to confirm it by saying, "I have rejoiced over my great wealth, the fortunes my hands have gained" (Job 31:25 NIV).

God gave Satan permission to try Job's faith. One day, his oxen and donkeys were taken, and his servants murdered by the Sabeans. His sheep and shepherds were burned up. The Chaldeans took his camels and murdered their caregivers. Then he found out that his seven sons and three daughters were in his oldest son's house when it collapsed and killed all ten of them. This all happened in one day!

A few days later, Satan "struck Job with terrible sores. Job had ulcers and scabs from head to foot. They itched and oozed so badly that he took a piece of broken pottery to scrape himself" (Job 2:7–8 MSG). It was bad. His wife wanted him to curse God, but he would not. He remained faithful while the script of his great life was being composed.

He kept his integrity, and when this massive storm was over, the Lord restored his health and wealth. "God blessed Job's latter life even more than his earlier life. He ended up with Fourteen thousand sheep, Six-thousand camels, one thousand teams of oxen, and one thousand donkeys. He also had seven sons and three daughters" (Job 42:12–13 MSG). God gave him back double everything. Even doubled his children since his first ten went to heaven. That's ten on earth and ten in heaven.

He lost so much and remained faithful to God. His experience serves as an example to us. If he can lose all that and still trust God, so can we. His trials are recorded in the Bible—the most read book of all times. What an assignment to have a record of your troubles for most of the known world to learn from.

Brothers Boaz and Job had huge wealth to fulfill their huge assignments. As a result, many people have been introduced to Christ and encouraged to get through their storm. Great wealth for the believer is determined by how many people you are supposed to benefit. Great wealth for me may not be the same as it is for you. I don't need the resources or the ability to get them like Bishop T. D. Jakes, Joel Osteen, or Pat Robertson. Not right now anyway. How much do you need to impact your section of the world? What's your capacity to benefit others like?

A NEW SEASON

How can I get and keep the resources I need to fulfill my assignment (the role that only I can play)? Having a high IQ will help, but some of the smartest people in the world are professors at universities, and they are notoriously bad with money. A high IQ doesn't guarantee great wealth. You could win a large sum of money from the lottery or have a deceased loved one's inheritance. That would help, but without changing your ways, you will soon need another large sum. You'll end up in the same position you were in before you got the money.

The only lasting solution is to apply God's financial instructions, "Honor God's commands and grow rich" (Proverbs 13:13 MSG). Anybody who has ever gotten and held on to wealth legally, whether they knew it or not, were honoring some of God's financial commands. There's no getting around it. God's word shows us all the corrections we need to make in our financial lives. It warns us that "poverty and shame will come to him who disdains correction, but he who regards a rebuke will be honored" (Proverbs 13:18 NKJV). To scorn correction brings poverty because wealth has to be acquired and kept intentionally. Being humble enough to embrace regular rebukes produces a life of honor. That's God's way.

A rebuke is a sharp reprimand. It's being told that you are wrong. You won't receive that unless you've had some of the pie. You can't have a great life unless you're willing to make constant course corrections. You see how your ways fall short of God's, and you determine how you can apply His wisdom to your situation. If you see that God asks for

10 percent of your income and you've been keeping it, then you receive it as a rebuke. Your ability to see every God rebuke as a door to a new season in your life will determine what new seasons you access. One rebuke with some pie can bring you what a hundred compliments will not, riches and honor.

Making it plain for us, God's Word declares, "By humility and the fear of the Lord are riches and honor and life" (Proverbs 22:4 NKJV). Humility and fear or reverence for God brings the things that make you rich and honorable into this life. Let's unlock God's word for our finances so we will know what He wants us to reverence.

REVERENCE POINT 1
GOD'S VIEW

The first thing for us to humbly reverence about God is His view on us having great wealth. For too long, many in the church have viewed wanting money as selfish. They think money is like a pizza pie. If you take a slice, then there's one less slice for someone who may need it more than you. That's not the case. There's more money in circulation today (though it's not as valuable as it has been) than ever. For you to have wealth is not to deprive others of it. There's enough money for the world to be wealthy. In the United States today, there are more than six hundred billionaires, as opposed to only fifteen billionaires in 1988. There is more money available than we can spend. Now everybody is not going to be a billionaire or even a millionaire, but everybody can be wealthy. Money is more like the ocean. It shifts around often, but it's never depleted. God knows that, and He intends to get some of the ocean to us, a piece of the financial pie.

King David wrote, "Let the Lord be magnified, who has pleasure in the prosperity of His servant" (Psalm 35:27 NKJV). Our economic well-being is a source of delight to God. He's gratified when His children are what Saint Paul describes as "robust in God; wealthy in every way, so that you can be generous in every way" (2 Corinthians 9:11 MSG). We're to have a great relationship with God and be successful in every area of our lives so we can be great givers. Then we will be a testament to how good of a dad God is. He says to us, "I am the Lord your God who teaches you to profit, who leads you by the way you should go" (Isaiah 48:17 NKJV). God has a standing invitation to teach us how to be wealthy, to lead us down the paths of economic success.

Before we can learn from Him, we must be conscious of His good will toward us. Wanting money is not bad, and there's enough of it to go around. This is so more lives can be touched by the Master, Jesus. It's not so we can get temporarily more comfortable with bigger and better things. No, it's so more sinners can be saved, more desolate people can be delivered, and more leaders can be trained. Money enlarges our fingerprint on the world. It does make the world go around, and God wants to keep it spinning.

You never have to wonder if God wants you to be blessed. Never doubt His goodness toward you, for the integrity of His word is never in question. He's not our genie in a bottle, waiting to fulfill our latest materialistic lust, but He does want us to look to Him for everything we need to be the greatest possible expression of ourselves. Elder Moses said, "You shall [earnestly] remember the Lord your God for it is He who gives you power to get wealth that He may establish His covenant" (Deuteronomy 8:18 AMP). Don't forget that He's enabling us to prosper so His will, His covenant, can be carried out on earth.

This is why Christians are to see everything they have as God's. If He asks for us to do something with it, then there is no pain attached to losing it. The only reason we don't like to give money is we see it as belonging to us and not to God. Thus, we think we won't be able to do what we could if we were to keep it all. I've heard it said like this, "We're to be stewards over all we have and owners of nothing." "The earth, after all, is God's, and everything in it" (1 Corinthians 10:26 MSG).

REVERENCE POINT 2
THE TITHE

The next thing we need to reverence about God is His desire for us to tithe on what we have. We see this when God asks the Israelites, "Do honest people rob God? Bu you rob me day after day. You ask, 'How have we robbed you?' The tithe and the offering—that's how" (Malachi 3:8 MSG)! God says we're some dishonest thieves when we don't give Him a tithe and an offering. The tithe is 10 percent of your increase, and an offering is anything above that. If at least 11 percent of your last paycheck wasn't given to God, then you're stealing from Him! He lets you rob Him, but in doing so, you rob yourself of His provision.

It's been estimated that only approximately 20 percent of churchgoers tithe. That means the other 80 percent are thieves. We have to be willing to be misunderstood by the thieving 80 percent if we're going to be a part of the provided for 20 percent.

God went on to tell the Israelites, "And now you're under a curse—the whole lot of you—because you're robbing me. Bring your full tithe to the temple treasury so there will be ample provisions in My temple. Test Me in this and see if I don't open up heaven itself to you and pour out blessings beyond your wildest dreams" (Malachi 3:9–10 MSG). When you tithe, God redeems the rest of your money from under the curse. He gives us the opportunity to participate in the blessing to honor Him by giving to Him the full tithe first. That attaches the blessing to what you have and empowers your finances to go as far as possible. It also gives God permission to give you more. Tithing is honoring God with your finances; it conveys your trust in Him. When you give the tithe with great faith attached to it, God says, "I'll make what you have left go further; I'll give you dreams, visions, and ideas to prosper you and your family."

I don't care if you make ten dollars an hour. Commit one of those ten first to your church or wherever you are being fed the Word of

God. "Honor God with everything you own; Give Him the first and the best" (Proverbs 3:9 MSG). Whenever I receive any money, whether it's a gift or earned, I don't start calculating how I'm going to spend 100 percent of it because it's not for my use only. I'm a steward of it all, so I appreciate what He lets me keep. I don't pay all my bills, plan for entertainment and shopping, and then see if I can squeeze out a tip for God. He's not a waitress!

He asks for the tithe and offering to reveal our hearts to ourselves so we can identify who we are really worshipping. The money trail doesn't lie.

TITHING TODAY? REALLY?

1. Most people don't tithe because they assume that it's counterproductive to the American dream, their piece of the pie. They think that to get great wealth, you have to keep every dime you can get your hands on. It doesn't make sense to them to live on less than 100 percent of their earnings. Min. Andrew Womack says we like to "get all we can, can all we get, then sit on our can." Yet God's kingdom is designed so that all roads lead back to Him. He has built Himself into the equation. He knows that money tends to make us forget about Him because it gives us the power to change our situation. In the natural, it's hard to fathom how giving away 10 percent of what I make helps me to achieve my goal of having more. That's why most people don't tithe. They learned in math class that you can't subtract from the whole and add to the sum at the same time. Yet that's exactly what God does. You might not see it immediately, but when you tithe in faith, increase is assigned to your finances.
2. Another reason people don't tithe is they think they don't make enough money to tithe. They are blinded by bills and other responsibilities. Every dime they have is already accounted

for. They can't afford it because bad financial decisions have everything tied up. Pride has us make many awful financial decisions just so we can appear wealthy, oftentimes for people who could care less. What do you do if the numbers won't let you tithe, even if you wanted to? You assess what you have and what you're paying on. See what you can get rid of. See where you can downsize because if you can't tithe, you're in over your head! Do you need all those cable channels, clothes, cars, or a house that big? With a little shifting around, you'll see that you can give ten dollars out of every hundred. You'll soon discover that you can't afford not to tithe because it's God's invitation to prosper you financially.

3. Finally, people don't tithe because they claim the church or preacher doesn't need their money. They don't trust their temple to use their treasure wisely. I know there's charlatans out there, but you leave them to God. Trust Him to have you give to the right house of God. The tithe will be to your credit even if they do spend it frivolously. Give because the house of God must have money to fulfill the will of God.

Usually, this exercise is often a crutch for believers who are uninterested in parting ways with their hard-earned money. So the curse (regular misfortune) remains on their finances because they remain thieves. The only thing you can do with the tithe is give it to God or steal it. To steal the tithe is to put yourself first.

You'll always be able to find a reason not to tithe. Your mind will tell you you're losing money that could be used to meet your needs. Yet great minds find a way to tithe. They always acknowledge that they wouldn't have a paycheck if it wasn't for God.

Father Abraham knew how to honor God. After a big payday in Sodom, Abraham's first move was to give his 10 percent to "Melchizedek King of Salem, priest of the Most High God" (Hebrews 7:1 NKJV). There's no evidence that God commanded him to. The Mosaic law wasn't given yet, but because Abraham was a friend of God's, he sensed God's longing for one tenth of his things. Tithing is saying, "God, this is Yours. Thank You for letting me keep the rest." He only asks for 10 percent. Uncle Sam asks for more than that, and he can't do for you what God can!

REVERENCE POINT 3
AN OFFERING

The next thing to reverence about God is His request for an offering. When the Israelites asked God how they could have possibly robbed Him, He not only told them that not tithing was stealing, but for His kids not presenting an offering with the tithe was stealing as well. He said they were disingenuous thieves because they kept "the tithe and the offering" (Malachi 3:8 MSG). Many Christians know that they should tithe, but not many trust God with more than that. Thus, they disconnect from the very thing they're trying to acquire—financial success.

An offering is an additional part of your money or possessions above the tithe. It's a tribute to God. He doesn't want all of your money; He wants you to cheerfully exceed the 10 percent requirement. The offering says, "God, You have my heart. This money will go further if I offer it to You." Curiously, all the secular literature I've read on "how to build wealth" tells you to be philanthropic. They all suggest giving on average 11 to 13 percent of your income to charity or a church. It's an echo of the timeless wisdom of God's Word, give beyond the tithe and live beyond the norm! Prioritize your giving. You decide what amount you want to offer. There's no set percentage, but it does have to be set aside. "God spoke to Moses 'Tell the Israelites that they are to set aside offerings for Me. Receive the offerings from everyone who is willing to give. These are the offerings I want you to receive from them: gold, silver, bronze, blue, purple, and scarlet material; fine linen; goat's hair; tanned ram's skins, dolphin skins; acacia wood, lamp oil; spices for anointing oils and for fragrant incense; onyx stones and other stones" (Exodus 25:1–7 MSG). God wants us to donate voluntarily. He asked Moses to collect from "everyone who is willing to give." He wants us to be generous with Him as an expression of His importance to us. We give to people we love. When we're involved with someone, we give to them and the people, systems, and organizations that would make them happy. When you love God, you will find an offering for Him. He removed all fixed-income or lack-of-money excuses. If you don't have silver or gold, then you can bring Him some spices and oils. Don't let what you don't have stop you from getting in on God's plan for your financial success.

His word is the trump card. It doesn't matter what the unemployment rate is, what the minimum wage is, or what the national debt is. He'll have you creating jobs or finding a better-paying one to help with the country's debt. Whatever the shape of the economy, He says, "Give, and you will receive. Your gift will return to you in full—pressed down, shaken together to make room for more, running over, and poured into your lap. The amount you give will determine the amount you get back" (Luke 6:38 NLT). That's His promise to us. If we will be uncommon givers, then we can be uncommon receivers. This goes for forgiveness, kindness, mercy, and goodness, as well as money.

We'll have to make room for the things that God wants to give us. Yet He's bound His generosity toward us to our willingness to be generous because more than anything, your use of money shows what you believe. Do you believe His word? Let me see how you use money, and I'll tell you if you believe it.

SEEDTIME AND HARVEST

This kind of giving beyond the tithe is also known in the scripture as "sowing seed." It's the law of seedtime and harvest. God said, "While the earth remains seedtime and harvest, cold and heat, winter and summer, and day and night shall not cease" (Genesis 8:22 NKJV). God says as long as there's an earth, attached to it will be twenty-four-hour periods, seasons, varying temperatures within the seasons, and the law of seedtime and harvest. It's why farming works. You put tomato seeds into the ground, and months later, tomato vines spring up. God's made the same law applicable to money; you "give and it will be given unto you" (Luke 6:38 NKJV). I heard Dr. Charles Stanley say it like this, "You reap what you sow, more than you sow, later than you sow." That goes for everyone; it's a universal law.

There is no day, season, or economic temperature that seedtime and harvest doesn't work in. You just have to plant the seed, have faith in God for a blessed return, and patiently wait on His word to come to pass. You can't plant a seed, and because you don't see an immediate harvest, you dig it back up. You would never reap any delicious tomatoes. Don't stop believing. When your harvest doesn't come in what you think is a timely manner, sow more seed. Know that God established this law for our benefit.

Naturally, there will be times when you will struggle to exceed the tithe. Humbly choose once to let God's rationale exceed yours. Do it one time, then reinforce your decision every time you're reluctant to give. You only have to make the decision once, then manage the decision. "Remember this – a farmer who plants only a few seeds will get a small crop. But the one who plants generously will get a generous crop" (2 Corinthians 9:6 NLT). That's God's heart for you. To "generously provide all you need. Then you will always have everything you need and plenty left over to share with others" (2 Corinthians 9:8 NLT). God wants His kids to always be able to say to those whom He wants to help, "Sure, I can help, I have plenty of God's resources left over."

Your money doesn't have to run out before the month does. Give the Father permission to invade your finances through the tithe and offering, and He will make sure you have seeds to sow. "For God is the one who provides seed for the farmer and then bread to eat. In the same way, He will provide and increase your resources and then produce a great harvest of generosity in you" (2 Corinthians 9:10 NLT).

The church at Philippi had a great harvest of generosity in them. During his first Roman imprisonment, the Apostle Paul received financial support from them. They liberally met his material needs. He wrote them, "I am generously supplied with the gifts you sent me with Epaphroditus. They are a sweet-smelling sacrifice that is acceptable and pleasing to God. And this same God that takes care of me will supply all your needs from His glorious riches, which have been given to us in Christ Jesus" (Philippians 4:8–19 NLT). They gave sacrificially, and God was going to make sure that they reaped what hey sowed. Their needs would be met from God's endless resource, "His glorious riches…in Christ Jesus." Our problem is that we think it's our responsibility to supply all of our own needs. Being our own god causes us to fail in letting God be God. He wants to be our supply. We just have to help the Apostle Paul that He's put in our lives.

I'm not advocating using this principle to get all we can, only giving because we want to have more. God wants us to have extravagant hearts, not hearts consumed with getting more money. For "those who love money will never have enough. How meaningless to think that wealth brings true happiness" (Ecclesiastes 5:10 NLT). The great children of God give, not in selfish manipulation for happiness but with an awareness that a byproduct of their giving is God's blessing. We're to be informed givers who are conscious of the faithfulness of God. That's what brings us happiness.

REFERENCE POINT 4
INVESTING

A lot of prosperity teaching stops there. God wants you to have great wealth, pay your tithes and offerings, and watch God do the rest. The scripture doesn't stop there though. After God told the Israelites He would bless them beyond their wildest dreams, then He tells them how He would do it. "For my part I will defend you against marauders, protect your wheat fields and vegetable gardens against plunderers" (Malachi 3:11 MSG). God's blessing was His protection of their harvest from the seeds they had already planted. They had made prior investments in wheat, barley, and other various vegetable seeds. They had something for God to bless. If their seeds had not have been in the ground, then they would not have had a harvest.

They didn't spend all their money on new designer clothes. Many of them went their whole lives without the luxury of a bath. It wasn't spent on transportation; they lived and conducted their business within a walking radius of their home. Their homes didn't cost a fortune. Many consisted of only a couple of rooms hosting multiple generations and animals. Entertainment and extravagant vacations didn't drain their budgets as they enjoyed each other's company. They made good use of their resources like a "faithful and wise steward" (Luke 12:42 NKJV). They were good investors.

To maximize your financial world, you must be a wise investor. I'm not suggesting that you have an extensive, diversified portfolio with stocks and bonds, gold, and real estate. You would have to be wealthy to invest at that level (if you are able to do that—great!). What I'm suggesting is spending less and finding places to put your money in or assets that will make you money. For example, CDs and mutual funds are available. There's ATM or vending machines or pressure washers for cleaning gutters and windows, or even old antiques that can be resold. The wealthy King Solomon advises, "Divide your investments among many places, for you do not know what risks might lie ahead" (Ecclesiastes 11:2 NLT). To invest in faith is to give God a channel through which to bless you.

Brothers Boaz and Job gave God such a channel. They both had money invested in farmland and livestock that accounted for most of their great wealth. They weren't just consumers; they took care of their property.

You might know God wants to bless you, so you tithe and sow your seeds, but you're afraid to invest. You've done what's right spiritually, but you're fearful when it comes to doing what's right practically. Generally speaking, investing represents a mindset that deals shrewdly with income by saving and having a great vision for your financial world. Saving is a discipline. God wants us to have as much joy in being patient and saving as we do in spending because saving conveys our trust in Him.

Saving is investing in the you of the future. It's money that's not already obligated to anything. We should have at least six months' income saved in addition to a six months' income emergency fund. Sounds like a lot, but cars break down and jobs lay off. Having a savings is wise. You can't have a mature savings account overnight, but you can decide to start one overnight.

It's been said that impulse buys (spending on the whim) make up 50 percent of all purchases. You're pressured to "buy now and save" or "buy one get one free" and forget your boring budget. Your budget is not a fun less concept; it's a wise, biblical one. We just have to change our perception. Jesus asks, "Who would begin construction of a building without first calculating the cost to see if there is enough money to finish it?" (Luke 14:28 NLT). Do you have enough money saved or not? We must budget so we can construct the building of our lives to His specifications. Great investors budget and save. God's plan is failproof.

ENTREPRENEURS

Brother Boaz and Job are also great entrepreneurial examples. They both worked for themselves. Their investing in land, animals, and seeds were for their own business. When their land and animals produced a harvest, it belonged to them, the owners. Being a business owner moves you from the wage system (earnings based on the value you bring to the hour) to the profit system (earnings based on what the entire business makes in the hour). When you're in the wage system, you're limited by your insight, skill set, and time. But an owner keeps the profit from every hour that the business produces.

Owning a brick and mortar or an online business will bring you more wealth than what your boss can. Most people know the profit system is superior to the wage system, but fear keeps them doing what they've done all their lives. No problem, to master the wage system, see chapter 4.

In either system, the only way to optimize your finances is to reverence how God views money. Give God your tithe and offering and invest a portion of what you have left over.

I've been an entrepreneur in the making for a while now. I remember a few years ago I was being sued along with three other parties for $1.3 million. I didn't have $5,000 to my name, so it might as well have been $1.3 billion! It wasn't looking good for us. In fact, a lawyer whom a family member consulted with told me to put any future assets in a loved one's name. In other words, I was going to have to pay my share of that lawsuit approximately $325,000.

Now during this time, I had God's perspective on money. I was faithfully tithing, sowing seeds, and I was doing some low-risk investing while expecting God to relieve me from this daunting financial burden. It was going to be a climb, but God's financial principles were being reverenced. A few short months after the initial proceedings, I received a letter from the presiding judge informing me that he had mistakenly failed to do some paperwork for me, so the lawsuit against me was being dismissed! It was a miracle! The other parties were left to defend themselves in this case. They would be drained of more time, energy, and money, but my release (harvest) would free me from further mental and financial hardship. I didn't have $1.3 million, but God's laws served to close the distance in my financial troubles. Hallelujah!

It was the pie that kept me sowing even when I didn't see a change. I was tithing when I didn't have a bank account and that lawsuit threatened my monetary future. Remember, the humble will do daily what the haughty will only do occasionally. They'll persistently practice the few principles of greatness. There aren't fifty secrets to greatness, only the mastery of a few.

- Perseverance (being driven)
- Meekness (being diplomatic)
- Brokenness (being detachable)

CAUTION

God wants us to be able to pay our medical expenses, yes, but if we can't, we should be able to say with Saint Paul, "I have learned in whatever stat I am, to be content" (Philippians 4:11 KJV). The pie births contentment. At the same time, the Father doesn't want us to be idle, neglecting His great wealth principles. He wants us to be content while activating His laws right where we are. "Committed and persistent work pays off; get rich quick schemes are ripoffs" (Proverbs 28:20 MSG).

There will never be a perfect time to start tithing. The enemy wants us to keep pushing our giving off into the distance because if you can give away money, you can give away anything. You'll be positioned for greatness. King Solomon was the richest man who ever lived. He encouraged us to be proactive. He observed "farmers who wait for perfect weather never plant. If they watch every cloud, they never harvest" (Ecclesiastes 11:4 NLT). Don't wait for the perfect time to apply God's principles; it will never come.

GIVE CAREFUL THOUGHT TO YOUR WAYS

Let's say you reverence the four points. God's view on money

1. Give the tithe
2. Give an offering
3. Gainful investing

But it seems like "you earn wages only to put them in a purse with holes in it. This is what the Lord Almighty says, 'Give careful thought to your ways'" (Haggai 1:6–7 NIV). You might be applying the principles, but have you left Humble Drive, the place that obedience is fulfilled? God has made it clear, "He who covers his sins will not prosper" (Proverbs 28:13 NKJV). Remember sin is the death agent. It will kill the financial life that you hope to have.

Disobedience is a seed sown in the opposite direction of the wealth you want to acquire. You can't cheat on your taxes or be dishonest with a bill collector in your business. You might get some money, but you won't be able to fully enjoy it for worrying how you're going to protect it and earn more.

"God takes care of all who stay close to Him. But He pays back in full those arrogant enough to go it alone" (Psalm 31:23 MSG). There are one of two places to live in life, close to Father God or the land of arrogance. It's humble pie or the pride of life. To be close to Him is to be taken care of by Him, to be who He wants you to be. That's greatness. The pie isn't the easiest pastry to digest, but it is the most rewarding to digest.

Reverence God's plan for great wealth, and you will get your piece of the financial pie. You won't go from being broke to millionaire status overnight, but you will be righting the ship and headed in the right direction.

YOUR PIECE OF THE PIE:
A GREAT DELIVERANCE

But God sent me ahead of you to preserve for you a remnant
on earth, and to save your lives by a great deliverance.

—Genesis 45:7 (NIV)

As a teenager, I was a chronic suboptimal decision maker. I was fifteen the weekend my family took a summer vacation at Emerald Point Outdoor Water Park in High Point, North Carolina. They have this massive zip line that's suspended about fifty feet above a huge twelve feet deep pool. Now even though I'm from the country where there's lakes and ponds, I can't swim. But I let my older cousin, who was all of seventeen years old at the time, talk me into getting on this infamous zip line attraction. As if the laws of buoyancy would be suspended, and I would float like a feather.

I don't remember being nervous while waiting in line, just hot and dry. That was about to change. We laughed and joked all the way up the stairs like we were professional divers. I remember being apprehensive when we reached the top, and I saw all that blue water, but I wasn't going to turn back now. I put my hands on those rigged metal handlebars and started my swing down the line. I immediately looked to my left at the lifeguard seated comfortably in his highchair and yelled, "I can't swim!" I held on like I knew what I was doing, until the zip line had taken me as far as I could go. I dropped into the water feet first. *Splash!*

Either the lifeguard didn't hear me or he assumed I was "crying wolf" because he didn't jump in right away. I was fighting to stay above water for what seemed like a lifetime, though it was only fifteen seconds or so. Finally, he spotted me, blew the whistle to stop the ride, then dove in to the rescue. Thank God he could swim.

My decision was foolish; it could have cost me my life. I knew I couldn't swim, float, or drank all that water. If I was going to make it through this, it wasn't going to be because of me. By myself, I was hopeless. On my own, I would have perished. No matter how much money I had, what good deeds I had done, or what laws I had kept, none of that mattered. Submersed in water and panicking on my way to drowning, I needed a great deliverance.

JOSEPH DIVES IN

The patriarch Jacob and his family were in great danger. There was no grain where they were in Canaan; thus, they were facing starvation. This was the beginning of a seven-year famine. Some widespread natural catastrophe must have occurred because "the famine was in all the lands, but in all the land of Egypt there was bread" (Genesis 41:5 NKJV). Though they didn't bring this on themselves like I did, they were starting to feel the conditions worsening. Father Jacob told his sons, "I've heard that there is food in Egypt. Go down there and buy some so that we can survive, and not starve to death" (Genesis 42:2 MSG). Ten of his sons set out for the land of Egypt. Giving the gravity of the situation, they knew their trip had to be a successful one.

Now their brother, "Joseph, was governor of all Egypt and in charge of selling grain to all the people, it was to him that his brothers came" (Genesis 42:6 NLT). Fifteen years prior, these same brothers took Joseph's coat and sold him to some Midianite traders for twenty pieces of silver. Thinking that they would never see him again, they butchered a goat and put its blood on his coat. They presented it to their father as if they didn't know what happened to him. Over the next thirteen years, Joseph would experience being a slave and a prisoner due to his brother's jealousy.

Now the tables had completely turned. He held their future in his hands, the very one whose destiny they thought they destroyed. The natural disaster, plus the treatment of their brother, had them in deep water. Something they couldn't control (the land), plus something they could (their pride) had them in a well looking up for a great deliverance. Be careful how you treat people. God has a way of turning the tables.

"When they arrived, they bowed before him with their faces to the ground" (Genesis 42: 6 NLT) because Joseph was the second most powerful man in the land next to Pharaoh. His position commanded their respect. They didn't recognize him probably because of his Egyptian attire and the time that had elapsed. I'm sure they weren't expecting him to be leading anything, even if he was still alive. But you can't drown potential. "Joseph recognized his brothers instantly, but he pretended to be a stranger and spoke harshly to them" (Genesis 42:7 NLT). I can't imagine what he must have felt in that moment. He probably replayed in his mind what his brothers had done to them and how that effected his parents. I can picture him being briefly paralyzed with this emotional flood.

Joseph gave them some resistance, withholding his help like the lifeguard watching me fight the water, then he dived in to his family's rescue. He gave his brothers brand-new clothes, though they had taken his. He gave them money, though they left him none to survive with. He sent his father "these gifts: ten donkeys loaded with Egypt's best products and another ten donkeys loaded with grain and bread provisions for his father's journey back" (Genesis 45:23 MSG).

No doubt Joseph had delivered them. Their lives had been spared. The brothers were amazed; they knew they didn't deserve his help. They must have felt sorrow, remorse, fear, and flat-out disbelief. In fact, after he revealed himself to them, he wept and asked them, "Is my father still living? But his brothers were not able to answer him because they were terrified at his presence" (Genesis 45:3 NIV). Their fear of revenge was justified; Joseph had the power to have them locked up, tortured, or even killed. Exploiting their sibling had caught up with them. It almost cost them their lives.

But to their surprise, he demolished their fears of revenge, saying, "Do not be distressed, and do not be angry with yourselves for selling me here because it was to save lives that God sent me ahead of you"

(Genesis 45:5 NIV). What great perception! He chose to gaze at God's providence during his years of suffering instead of his wounds.

Joseph explained to his brother what God had revealed to him; that there would be five more years of famine he shared his thoughts. "God sent me ahead of you to preserve for you a remnant on earth, and to save your lives by a great deliverance" (Genesis 45:7 NIV). They would've been greatly defeated if Joseph hadn't saved them. Operating at greatness as the governor of Egypt positioned him to save them by rendering a great deliverance. Do you need saving of some sort? God sent me ahead of you to preserve for you a piece of your pie!

SIZABLE SAVING

A deliverance is the act of delivering or saving to rescue from danger or difficulty. You can advance your career, expand your vision, develop your mind, increase your faith, grow in power, extend your leadership, and multiply your wealth. But at some point, you're going to need delivering. It's impossible to account for all the dangers and difficulties that life will bring.

It could be a terminal illness, a sudden car accident, chronic depression, or bondage to drugs and alcohol. These miseries and afflictions are massive in danger and difficulty. They are great odds to overcome; therefore, they require a great deliverance. When you have no hope in the natural, you need supernatural help. That's God's part; He can get whatever help you need to you,

whether you're in fifteen feet of water and can't swim or you're drowning in a famine and your food supply has run out. It could be a dumb decision on your part or a catastrophe of not doing your own. Either way, you're going to need a number of sizable savings before you die.

A DELIVERER

God always has somebody prepared with the necessary resources, connections, know-how, and power to do for you what you can't do for yourself. Even when God divinely intervenes with a miracle and there appears to be no human intervention, it's because He has heard the prayer of some righteous one. An intercessor praying in agreement with the will of God for a breakthrough. The righteous have the earth covered in delivering prayer.

Moses was a righteous deliverer. The Bible called him a "deliverer by the hand of the Angel who appeared to him in the bush" (Acts 7:35 NKJV). "Othniel the son of Kenaz, Caleb's younger brother" (Judges 3:9 NKJV) was called a deliverer. "Ehud the son of Gera, the Benjamite, a left-handed man" (Judges 3:15 NKJV) was one too. Moses was a spiritual man. Othniel wasn't famous; he was known because of his brother's courage. Ehud was from a small family, and he was left-handed, psychically different from the mases. No matter what type you need or where you need it from, God has a great deliverer in place for you. He is going to answer your prayer at the right time when the maximum amount of people are benefited, and the least amount of people are sorrowed.

SALVATION

At the right time, the Father provided a hero for our great spiritual danger. He's the Deliverer form Zion, the Lord Jesus Christ. Because of Adam and Eve's sin, everyone who has entered the world since has entered it under the curse of sin. Hell, eternal separation from God is the inevitable destination. It's the real living dead where your spirit continues to exist without its Maker. Since there is no relationship with God, hell is simply existing without the possibility of obtaining greatness. Heaven is eternity spent with greatness; hell is eternity spent without it.

Once we reach the age of accountability—being old enough to make a conscious decision to walk with God—we instantly become doomed to hell. We are destined for great evil unless we accept God's great deliverer. We've heard of the splendor of heaven full of God's presence; it's only matched by the awfulness of hell that's completely void of His presence.

In their book, *The Bible Has the Answer*, Dr. Morris and Martin Clark says,

> Essentially, hell is the place where all aspects of the presence of God will be completely withdrawn forever… Thus in Hell there will be no love, for God is love. There will be no light, for God is light and in Him is no darkness at all. There will be no peace, or rest or joy, since these are all attributes of God. On the contrary, there will be eternal corruption, strife, rebellion and hatred.

None of our good works can keep us away from being permanent residents in this place. We can't keep enough laws, perform enough deeds, or give enough money. The debt is too great. Only a significant payment would successfully satisfy condemned man's sin debt. That's who Jesus is "the Lamb of God who takes away the sin of the world" (John 1:29 NKJV). He was God's Deliverer that with His life more than compensated for our debt. Everyone may not realize it, but all need this new life to escape that old death. God knows we are hopeless non swimmers who are starving and about to perish. So excelling at the right thing, at the right place, at the right time, Jesus dived onto the scene.

My dear friend, based on the reliability of God's Word, your eternal destiny can be taken care of now, if you haven't done so yet. Repent of your offenses with both God and man and confess your confidence in Jesus. It is the greatest decision you'll ever make because "He will beautify the humble with salvation" (Psalm 149:4 NKJV).

MORE SAVING

God engineered the master plan that salvation is, so certainly anything that we need to be saved from now is within His ability to engineer. In fact, during the greatest catastrophe in the history of the world (a global flood), God was not taken by surprise. "The Lord sat enthroned at the flood" (Psalm 29:10 NKJV). The world was in its greatest danger, but God was there saving Noah and his family.

More sizable saving is going to be required before you encounter heaven's bliss because more danger and difficulty are ahead. And like Noah, other people are connected to your destiny. They need you to get and stay delivered from whatever it is that has you limited or bound. Operation rescue won't be called off until we get to heaven.

THE PIE, THEN CRY

Down here, all rescues are scheduled to take place on Humble Drive. Then when we get there, God's waiting to hear us cry out to Him. King David records God saying, "Call to me and I'll answer, be at your side in bad times, I'll rescue you, then throw you a party. I'll give you a long life, a long drink of salvation" (Psalm 91:15–16 MSG). Wow, God is longing to throw us an after-the-rescue party. He wants to celebrate the humble that has requested and received that "long drink of salvation."

After I had swallowed some of that chlorine water during my zip line accident, I was thirsty for a drink of salvation. So standing on the side of the pool after my rescue felt like a party. I was celebrating the fact that I was still alive! It didn't matter that I was slightly embarrassed and banned from the ride; I was safe and secure. That's what God wants to provide for us—safety and security during life's troubles and hell when we die. King David echoed this when he declared that God was his "refuge in the day of my trouble" (Psalm 59:16 NKJV).

That's the confidence I had in the lifeguard's ability to get me out of those deadly waters before I even got in them. David had the same trust. He knew God would answer him and be by his side even before he needed Him. You can trust God to deliver you out of any sinking situation. I heard Pastor Joel Osteen say that "greatness will get you out of a great mess."

Brother Peter had his own run-in with a pool of water. One day, the disciples were in a boat. "They were battered by the waves. At about four o'clock in the morning" (Matthew 14:24–25 MSG). Jesus came near them, walking on the water. Peter knew that he could trust Jesus, so he asked for His permission to walk on the water. His request was granted, so he hopped out of the boat and made his way toward Jesus. He was doing well until his perspective shifted. He looked down and saw the ragging waves. This caused his faith to waver, then he started to sink. Just like me, he couldn't overcome the water on his own. However, he knew his help was just a cry away. "He cried out 'Master save me!' Jesus didn't hesitate. He reached down and grabbed his hand" (Matthew 14:30 MSG). There is no indecision in the Lord Jesus; His mind is permanently set to save.

A couple years ago, I taught on God's delivering power. It was a Wednesday night. I gave the altar call, and everyone there came forward! Sensing the heart of God in that moment, I prayed for the cancellation of any bad seeds sown. I prayed that God would deliver His people from any great debts, dangers, or difficulties limiting them. There were many testimonies from that service.

One of them involved my friend. I didn't know it, but he had a debt of over thirty thousand dollars that he had incurred years ago. It was owed to his ex-wife, and he was content with making payments on it, but God had other plans. The next morning, he called his sister who informed him that his ex-wife had called her saying that she was dropping the case against him. She explained that he could call the courthouse to confirm it. The Lord had moved on her heart the very moment that we prayed! The great debt was canceled. No more worrying about how he was going to pay it off. I joined in with his cry from the pickup spot, and the next morning, he received word of his great deliverance.

PRAISE TO PRECEDENCE

One way to cry out to God is to praise Him. He'll take that call every time. A praise is an expression of admiration or warm approval, a strong commendation. To praise is to recognize the greatness of another. David said, "Let me shout God's name with a praise song, let me tell His greatness in a prayer of thanks" (Psalm 69:30 MSG). When you need a situation flooded with greatness, give God your warm approval, adoration, and strong commendation. He will pick the phone up.

There was a time when the people of Moab, Ammon, and Mount Seir came to make war with Jehoshaphat, king of Judah, for their land. They joined forces in En Gedi. Despite his fears, the king responded in the right way. He "set himself to seek the Lord, and proclaimed a fast throughout Judah" (2 Chronicles 20:3 NKJV). His first move was to get to Humble Drive, then he asked all of Judah to get there with him by fasting. When you are opposed by a great number of people, it's wise to get your allies invested in your victory.

King Jehoshaphat was serious about his responsibility to protect his people. In prayer, he praised, "O Lord God of our fathers, are You not God in heaven, and do You not rule over all the kingdoms of the nations, and in Your hand is there not power and might, so that no one is able to withstand You? Are You not our God who drove out the inhabitants of Abraham, Your friend forever?" (2 Chronicles 20:6–7 NKJV). The king was admiring God, then he brought up God's track record. Since He gave that land to His friends, those nations would have to get their own real estate.

From that national atmosphere of prayer and praise, a young man named Zechariah commanded the people of Judah to "not be afraid nor dismayed because of this great multitude, for the battle is not yours, but God's" (2 Chronicles 20:15 NKJV). Notice they didn't confess (pretend) that this huge problem wasn't in front of them. Zechariah was just shifting their attention back to God because He claimed ownership of the battle. Their job in the fight was to trust God. Their praise would be an expression of that trust. The king appointed a choir and sent them out in front of the army. They started to cry out, "Praise the Lord, for His mercy endures forever. Now when they began to sing and to praise, the Lord sent ambushes against the people of Ammon, Moab, and Mount Seir, who had come against Judah and they were defeated" (2 Chronicles 20:21–22 NKJV). Judah's foes became their own adversaries. That's how God delivered them from all the troops.

Before this deliverance, no nation had been delivered because its opponents had turned on each other. There was no reference point for this kind of victory. Do not back what God is going to do for you on the experiences of others. It doesn't matter how bad it looks for you or how long you've been in your situation. God is a precedential God.

The Bible is a book about God setting precedence. No one had been saved from floodwaters in an ark until Noah and his family were. No woman had ever been delivered from barrenness at ninety-year-old until Sarah was. No nation had been freed from slavery because some plagues were released until Israel was. No man had exited a fiery furnace or a lion's den before Daniel did. And no man had ever come back from being scourged and crucified until Jesus did. God is a precedential God!

BROKENNESS

Because of his precedential record, God asked the Israelites two rhetorical questions, "Do I bring to the moment of birth and not give delivery? says the Lord. Do I close up the womb while I bring to delivery? says your God" (Isaiah 66:9 NIV). While you're waiting for your breakthrough, your praise will bring you to your moment of birth. Stay broken; God is going to get the glory. Interestingly, the Hebrew word Isaiah uses for the phrase "moment of birth" is *shabor*. It's translated in six other places in the Old Testament as broken. *Shabor* describes a "breaking of or breaking forth. It's pictured as giving birth" (Dr. James Strong). I want God's children to know that when you're broken, you're in the birthing position. You are close to your "moment of birth." Your moment of delivery is at hand. An idea is coming any day now; a financial miracle, a miraculous release, a great deliverance is on the way. It hurts to be broken, but it's necessary for a delivery. We only sense the pain, the hurt, the emptiness of needing to be saved. Yet the broken are simultaneously breaking forth into a new season.

King Jehoshaphat had gotten himself and Judah in the birthing position. Their fasting produced a praise, and a great deliverance ensued. Don't think you're wiser than God that you can figure your life out on your own. You need a deliverer, and God is still in the delivering business!

CAUTION

After you've received a great deliverance, make sure you keep your warm approvals for God and not yourself. We'll start admiring our minds, our skill sets, our money, our organizations, even our prayers if we don't watch it. Praise can turn inward quickly. That's why we are to "let another man praise you and not your own mouths" (Proverbs 27:2 NKJV). That is what happened to Lucifer (now known as Satan) in heaven. He used to be one of God's lead praisers until he had to go because he started praising himself. He is still a praiser; he just praises himself now. Caution—praise without the pie is disgusting self-admiration. Self-praise will cause you to fail.

God's hand is ever stretched out toward us, but to connect to His assistance, you have to honor Him continuously with the fruit of your lips. When I don't get the deal I was hoping for, when debt is inevitable, or cancer has just been discovered, remember King David's declaration, "I will praise the Lord at all time, I will constantly speak His praises. I will boast only in the Lord; let all who are helpless take heart. Come let us tell of the Lord's greatness; let us exalt his name together" (Psalm 34:1–3 NLT). In the seams of life, whenever my mind drifts away from the awareness of God, I "speak His praises." When all is well, I will resist self-righteousness, the temptation to praise myself. I will boast only in the Lord. That's the example for the hopeless. Be found with those that don't mind telling of the greatness of the Lord. He's "enthroned in the praises of" (Psalm 22:3 NKJV) His people. He takes a seat in praise. It's how we get close to Him, and the closer we get to Him, the closer we get to our great deliverance.

THE OPTIMAL LIFE PIE

Remember "some people dig a fork into the pie but are too lazy to bring it to their mouth" (Proverbs 19:24 MSG). Is that you or will you do daily what the haughty only does occasionally? Are you driven to God, diplomatic with people, and ever detaching from offending both God and people? Will you let God get as much glory as possible from you so you can be as impactful and fulfilled as you can be? Are you ready to excel at the right thing, at the right place, and at the right time so the maximum amount of people will benefit and the least amount of people sorrowed? If you are, then you will get a piece of the optimal life pie.

Now we drift in and out of greatness (situationally and seasonally). Thus, I'm constantly asking God, "How can you get the most glory out of this situation?" That's significance. I'm constantly evaluating the moment and reading the people so I can maximize my influence. That's success. Then I find rest in the fulfillment of the Lord. That's satisfaction.

Remember that all temptation is an attempt to get you off of

Brokenness Boulevard, Humble Drive, Humility Avenue. Satan wants you to abort your destiny. Don't be lazy. Keep a fork full of the pie coming to your mouth. A great life is yours, a great career, a great vision, a great mind, great faith, great power, great leadership, great wealth, and a great deliverance. Know that humility is a mere prelude to your piece of the pie!

REFERENCES

King James Version (KJV). Copyright © 1982 by Thomas Nelson, Inc.

New King James Version (NKJV). Copyright © 1982 by Thomas Nelson, Inc.

New International Version (NIV). Copyright © 1973, 1978, 1984 by International Bible Society.

English Standard Version (ESV). Copyright © 2001 by Crossway.

The Message (MSG). Copyright © 1993, 1994, 1995, 1996, 2000, 2001, 2002 by NavPress Publishing Group.

New Living Translation (NLT). Copyright © 1996, 2004 by Tyndale House Publishers.

Amplified Bible (AMP). Copyright © 1954, 1958, 1962, 1964, 1965, 1987 by The Lockman Foundation.

Complete Jewish Bible (CJB). Copyright ©1998 by Jewish New Testament Publications.

The New Strong's Expanded Exhaustive Concordance of The Bible – Red Letter Edition. Copyright © 2001 by Thomas Nelson Publishers.

Stanley, Charles F. *30 Life Principles*. 2007. Atlanta, Georgia: Intouch Ministry.American Heritage College Dictionary, Third Edition. 1993. Houghton Mifflin Company.Clark, Martin, and Dr. Henry Moss. 1976. *The Bible Has the Answer*. Green Forest, AR: Master Books.Maxwell, John. 2008. *Leadership Gold*. Nelson.

ABOUT THE AUTHOR

Dr. C. S. Wilson is the cofounder of myeventadvisor.com. He is an emotional breakthrough expert and a highly sought-after speaker. With a heart calibrated to the heart of God, he seeks to help people create systems, delete sorrows, and increase sales. His wit is a gift to mankind.

CPSIA information can be obtained
at www.ICGtesting.com
Printed in the USA
LVHW081332261020
669842LV00014B/1039